THE
GOODNESS
OF GOD

DR. DAN C. HAMMER

Unless otherwise noted, Scripture quotations are from the New Spirit Filled Life Bible, Thomas Nelson Publishing Company, 2002. Used by permission. All rights reserved.

Printed in the United States of America

First Publication: September 2015

ISBN #978-1517613297

Ordering Information: danhammerministries@isonrise.org
Ministry information available at www.isonrise.org
Special discounts are available on quantity purchases.
Contact: bookstore@isonrise.org

DEDICATION

I dedicate this book to God the Father, Jesus Christ the Son and the Holy Spirit. I am so thankful to God for all the love and goodness He has lavished on me. His loving kindness is beyond words.

My desire as God has taken me on a journey of revealing His goodness is to release the goodness of God to everyone I see. God is so good!!!

ACKNOWLEDGMENTS

I thank God for His goodness in giving me my wife, Terry, my sons and daughter in laws, John and Grace, David and Darcie, my daughter Anna and for my four grandchildren Hailey, Emma, Justus and Addison.

I am so thankful for the elders, staff and church family of Sonrise Christian Center. They have been an extension of God's goodness to me.

Thank you to Patricia Burke, Heidi Widell, Tara Johnson and Debby Werdell for all their technical help with this book.

Also, thank you to my friend Leif Hetland for writing the foreword to this book.

See, Receive and Release the Goodness of God!!!

ENDORSEMENTS

This book is good. It is very good! A few years ago, Dr. Dan Hammer was with us in Alabama. He ministered to our congregation on "The Goodness of God." I vividly remember the message and how powerfully anointed it was. God used it to align us more fully with His loving heart. To this day, people still mention the message that Pastor Dan preached about goodness. I am so happy that this book, which carries one of the most powerful revelations I have ever heard, has now been birthed.

You too will be impacted as you experience the drawing power of this revelation. The Holy Spirit will lead your heart more and more toward the Father's true heart of goodness; you will be transformed by the testimonies and truths you will encounter. This revelation is a mind-shifter and a heart-shaper. Dr. Dan's personal history with God, his Spirit-birthed insight into the Scripture and his own passion for Jesus has resulted in this powerful treatise of goodness. As you begin the journey through these pages, get ready to become overwhelmed with the goodness of God.

Eddie Lawrence, D.Min.
Senior Pastor of Grace House
Florence, Alabama

There are times when God seems to highlight one of the majestic aspects of His character and right now He is revealing to us His goodness in greater measure. Dr. Dan Hammer turns a floodlight on the many facets of God's goodness in such a way that we receive not only a greater understanding of it, but also the ability to embrace His goodness for ourselves and others. You will be blessed as you read this wonderful book.

Jane Hansen Hoyt
President/CEO
Aglow International

CONTENTS

FOREWORD

Five years ago I was part of a conference together with my friend Dan Hammer. He preached a message that the Holy Spirit used in a powerful way. Sitting in the front of Sonrise Christian Center waves of Papa God's goodness came over me. At that moment I knew in my heart that the next major move sweeping across America and touching the nations will all start with believers who would receive, become and release his goodness.

A healthy Christian life cannot exist without each of us having a fresh revelation of how much Papa God loves us and that it is His will to lavish us with goodness and kindness.

The author is authentic, anointed and appointed to impart to you a message that he has become. You teach what you know but reproduce who you are. Kindness and goodness is living a lifestyle of Jesus, anointed by the Holy Spirit and bringing glory to the Father. Anyone who gets close to you and His goodness will be powerfully touched by God. Bodies healed, marriages restored, businesses prosper and Hindus, Muslims and other hungry people will taste and see that God is good.

Jesus lived with an awareness that his Papa was good and released a gospel that touched and transformed every person that got close to him. Terrorist Saul became the Apostle Paul, Zacchaeus the chief tax collector became the generous giver to the poor, lepers cleansed, the blind see, hope restored, the dead raised – all as an act of the kindness and goodness of God.

That same lifestyle is what I see spreading all over the world. I call it a goodness virus and it is highly contagious. Nobody can resist this extravagant goodness and kindness that targets everyone in need for some love. God's love!

It is with honor and joy that I highly recommend for you and I to join Dan Hammer and Sonrise Christian Center to receive a lifestyle of goodness and kindness that will touch our families, churches, workplaces and eventually every person around us. They will experience acts of goodness and kindness that will lead to repentance.

The world is about to see we are his disciples by the way we love one another. This love is something we first receive before we release. My own journey since that day five years ago in Seattle has become my lifestyle. I do not know how many people have been saved nor how many lives have been touched. I do know the goodness of God and a lifestyle of goodness will change the world.

Buy two copies of this book, one for you and a friend that will become your goodness partner. Practice His presence and let this book be your easy guide.

One billion souls are waiting for us to enter His goodness and become change agents of kindness.

Leif Hetland
Author
Seeing Through Heavens Eyes

SECTION ONE
Seeing His Goodness

SEEING THE GOODNESS OF GOD
SEEING THE GOODNESS IN REPENTANCE
SEEING THE GOODNESS OF GOD AS MOSES DID
SEEING THE GOODNESS OF GOD IN CREATION
SEEING THE GOODNESS OF GOD FOLLOWING US
SEEING THE GOODNESS OF GOD AHEAD IN HOPE

Psalm 16:2, "O my soul, you have said to the Lord, 'You are my Lord, my goodness is nothing apart from You.'"

The Psalmist understood that our goodness is nothing apart from the Lord. I often say, "Any good thing you see in me is because of Him." He is so full of goodness. As a matter of fact, Psalm 33:5 says, "He loves righteousness and justice; the earth is full of the goodness of the Lord."

"The word 'goodness' in the Greek is *agathosune* which means goodness, i.e., virtue or beneficence, goodness. It comes from a root word that means an intrinsic goodness rather than an outward appearance."[1]

We have a choice to live life seeing the goodness of the Lord and focusing on Him or seeing the evil and darkness. Don't misunderstand! We all see evil and live in a fallen world, but we can BE GOOD NEWS if we focus our eyes, mind and heart on God and His goodness. The earth is full of the goodness of God – LOOK FOR IT!

---

1 The Spirit-Filled Life Bible, (NKJV), Thomas Nelson, Nashville, TN, Jack Hayford, General Editor footnote, (©2002), pg. 1573.

CHAPTER ONE

Seeing the Goodness of God

I was born at Madigan Army Hospital, Fort Lewis, Washington, October 4, 1953, to Dr. Frank and Margaret Hammer. My mother died suddenly in a tragic car accident when I was six years old. Her death had a huge impact on my life and taught me to have a healthy respect for people who experience loss and death. After living a stereotypical American life in the 1950s and '60s I developed a sinful lifestyle that included drugs, alcohol and everything that comes with it. On August 11, 1975 at the age of 21, I surrendered my heart to the Lord Jesus Christ in Appleton, Wisconsin. That day I started my journey as a follower and disciple of Jesus Christ. I began a journey of seeing and receiving the goodness of God. God has been so good to me! I want everyone to see His goodness and receive it as I did that day in Appleton!

Let's begin with my first encounter with God's goodness in my life. By the time I turned 21 years old, my life had deteriorated and I had a nervous breakdown. My sin, fears, guilt and my shame had caught up with me. I tried to deaden my pain by using drugs and alcohol. What I pushed down for years from the death of my mother could no longer be ignored. Now, all my emotions and hurts began to surface. I was overwhelmed.

Little did I know how my sin and lifestyle had opened me up to the demonic realm.

In 1975 I was living with my sister, Laurel. One morning as I watched an NBA basketball playoff game I heard a voice say, "You are going to go crazy." From then on and for many months I struggled with depression, fear phobias and could not cope with everyday life. I would sometimes wake up and cry all day, not knowing why I was crying. Other days I would wake up with my heart beating so fast I thought I was dying of a heart attack. During those months, fear controlled my life and dominated all my thoughts.

My mother was a Christian and somehow after her death I ended up with her Bible. Amidst the fear and depression on one occasion I picked up her Bible and the first scripture I read was Matthew 9:12-14, "When Jesus heard that, He said to them, 'Those who are well have no need of a physican, but those who are sick. But go and learn what this means: 'I desire mercy and not sacrifice.' For I did not come to call the righteous, but sinners, to repentance.'" When I read this, my heart was convicted. All my life I thought Jesus had come for the "good people," but He said He came for the sick and the sinners, a category I solidly fit into. This shattered my image of what Christianity was – this was God's revelation to me. He loved me. How good was that?!

A few days later I opened my mother's Bible again and read what the Apostle Paul wrote in 2 Corinthians 12:9,10, "And He said to me, 'My grace is sufficient for you, for My strength is made perfect in weakness.' Therefore most gladly I will rather boast in my infirmities, that the power of Christ may rest upon me. Therefore I take pleasure in infirmities, in reproaches, in needs, in persecutions, in distresses, for Christ's sake. For when I am weak, then I am strong."

This verse about the Apostle Paul dealing with his thorn in the flesh caused me to realize that as weak as I was, Paul was saying God's strength could be made perfect in my weakness. I did not even know at the time who the Apostle Paul was! Not as I do now. But I heard he was the greatest Christian that ever lived. So suddenly there was a tiny little light shining in my dark heart.

In the process of mulling over these two verses and having the Holy Spirit work on my heart, I thought maybe God could help me! I was still struggling with fear, depression and all related things, as well as the spiritual torment of the enemy on my soul.

In the summer of 1975 I decided to go on vacation to my grandparent's house in Wisconsin with my sister, brother and a friend. I thought I would try and "get away from it all." Maybe a change of scenery would help. While on that vacation I had a familiar episode of panic attacks and depression. I was eating lunch and started to feel sick to my stomach. I went upstairs to the bathroom and vomited. I felt as if I couldn't take it anymore. I looked up to heaven and said, "God! If this is what being alive is, I don't want to live anymore." At that moment I heard a voice say, "Go read a book." I thought, "What is that going to do? All the people I've seen and books I've read to this point have not helped me at all!" Other voices I heard told me I was going to die, go crazy and then over and over again, "You can't take it anymore," seemed to shout out loud inside of me. Before I knew it I found myself walking down the stairs looking for a book and wondering why I was listening to the one positive Voice I was hearing!

Then I found it. On a bookshelf in the family room there was one book laying on top of all the others on the shelf. My heart was drawn straight to it. *The Cross and the Switchblade*, by David Wilkerson. Because of all I had been through at this point, I could understand the Psalmist in Psalm 16 when he spoke to his soul and said to the Lord, "You are my Lord, my goodness is nothing apart from You." Any good thing in me is because of Him. I had not yet received Jesus Christ to be my Lord and Savior, but He was working on me.

How good God was to have my mother's Bible there for me in my time of need. How good was Jesus to speak in my heart as the Voice of the Good Shepherd. How good was God to have the book by David Wilkerson in my grandparents' house on their bookshelf.

God Will Meet You with the Blessings of His Goodness

In Psalm 21:1-4, the psalmist David said, "The king shall have joy in Your strength, O Lord; and in Your salvation how greatly shall he rejoice! You have given him his heart's desire, and have not withheld the request of his lips. Selah. For You meet him with blessings of goodness; You set a crown of pure gold upon his head. He asked life from You, and You gave it to him – Length of days forever and ever." In verse 3 God is meeting David with the blessings of His goodness. God wants to meet us all with the blessings of His goodness. In your "meetings" with God, expect for Him to meet you with the blessings of His goodness. Now that's a good meeting! For those of you who have never met with God, He wants to meet with you and share His heart for you.

Deuteronomy 28 tells what blessings will come to those who *"diligently obey the voice of the Lord your God…"*

God will set you high above the nations of the earth (verse 1).

His blessings shall come upon you and overtake you (v. 2).

You will be blessed in the city and the country (v. 3).

God will bless the fruit of your body, your produce and lands (v. 4).

God will bless your kneading bowl and basket (v. 5).

You will be blessed when you come in and go out (v. 6).

God will cause your enemy to flee seven ways (v. 7).

God will command His blessings on your storehouses and all to which you set your hand (v.8).

God will establish you as a holy people to Himself (v.9).

All the peoples of the earth will be afraid of you (v.10).

The Lord will bless you with fruit, livestock and land (v.11).

You shall lend to nations and not borrow (v.12).

The Lord will make you the head and not the tail and above not beneath (v.13).

These will be some of the blessings with which you can expect God to demonstrate His goodness to you, child of God. If you are not yet His child I will explain at the end of the book how you can meet with God and become His child.

Reflect on how good God has been to you. How has He shown you His goodness? Remember the earth is full of the goodness of the Lord.

The blessings of God's goodness like those in Deuteronomy 28:1-14 can overtake you.

Reflect and Discuss

How He is meeting you with the blessings of His goodness?

CHAPTER TWO

Seeing the Goodness of God in Repentance

Romans 2:4, "Or do you despise the riches of His goodness, forbearance, and longsuffering, not knowing that the goodness of God leads you to repentance?"

That day on August 11, 1975 in Appleton, Wisconsin at my grandparents I read The Cross and the Switchblade. After I read it I opened my heart to Christ as my Lord and Savior. It was God's goodness that led me to repent. What is repentance? What does it mean that the goodness of God leads me to repent?

The word repentance in the Greek is metanoia, which means "a change of mind." This change of mind and heart brings about a change in life. It means you or I were going one way or direction and we turn to go another way - God's way. God in His goodness leads us to repent by convicting our heart. He is so kind and loving to show us our need of His love and forgiveness. In 2 Corinthians 7:10, "For godly sorrow produces repentance leading to salvation, not to be regretted; but the sorrow of the world produces death." God lovingly convicts us of our sin by the Holy Spirit's work in our heart.

Speaking of the Holy Spirit, in John 16:8-11 it says, "And when He has come, He will convict the world of sin, and of judgment: of sin, because they do not believe in Me; of righteousness, because I go to My Father and you shall see Me no more; of judgment, because the ruler of this world is judged." God's goodness leads us to repent and turn to Him just as I did on August 11, 1975. He is so good to begin to work on our heart to show us life isn't working without Him. It is His goodness that leads us to repent. He touches our heart and changes our heart and mind in His goodness.

Repentance Steps

1) Repentance is turning from sin and selfishness to God. I turn from controlling my life to yielding control to God through the work of Jesus Christ on the cross. "In the New Testament the English verb 'to repent' is normally used to translate the Greek verb metanoein. This Greek verb metanoein has one definite meaning throughout the history of the Greek language, right through classical Greek down to New Testament Greek. Its basic meaning is always the same: 'to change one's mind.' Thus 'repentance' in the New Testament is not an emotion, but a decision."[2]

2) As we repent we do what is found in Mark 1:15. "The time is fulfilled, and the Kingdom of God is at hand. Repent, and believe in the gospel." We change our minds and believe the good news about Jesus. We believe in Jesus. This same principle is seen in Acts 20:20,21 as the Apostle Paul speaks, "How I kept back nothing that was helpful, but proclaimed it to you, and taught you publicly and from house to house, testifying to Jews, and also to Greeks, repentance toward God and faith toward our Lord Jesus Christ." God's goodness leads us to change our minds and put faith toward our Lord Jesus Christ.

3) Repentance is something that continues in our Christian life on earth wherever our thinking does not line up with the

2 The Spirit-Filled Believer's Handbook, Derek Prince, Derek Prince Ministries, International Creation House, (©1993), pg. 100.

thinking of Jesus. We need to repent and think like Him. In Isaiah 55:8,9, "For My thoughts are not your thoughts, nor are your ways My ways,' says the Lord. 'For as the heavens are higher than the earth, so are My ways higher than your ways, and My thoughts than your thoughts.'" God wants to give us His thoughts - they're higher than others! Remember in Romans 2:4 it says not to despise the riches of His goodness, forbearance and long-suffering. He is rich in it! It is God's goodness that leads us to the doorway of repentance.

Kenneth S. Wuest a renowned Greek scholar said, "'Goodness' is chrēstotēs, 'benignity, kindness.' 'Forbearance' is anonchē, 'a holding back.' In classical Greek mostly of a truce of arms. It implies something temporary which may pass away under new conditions. Hence used in connection with the passing by of sins before Christ (Romans 3:25). 'It is that forbearance or suspense of wrath, that truce with the sinner, which by no means implies that the wrath will not be executed at the last; nay, involves that it certainly will, unless he be found under new conditions of repentance and obedience' (Trench)' (Vincent). Denney says: 'The goodness of God summarizes all three (goodness, forbearance, long-suffering) in the concrete.'"[3]

As a result of Christ's death and resurrection God has offered to us forgiveness for our sins. His goodness can lead us to repent of our sin and turn to Him. God's ultimate love on the cross brings His goodness to us.

A Journey of Change

The Christian life is a journey. Along the excursion there are opportunities to repent (change our mind) to think as Jesus Christ thinks, which He demands of us. If we do not think the way Jesus thinks, we need to change our mind. Colossians 3:1,2 says, "If then you were raised with Christ, seek those things which are above, where Christ is, sitting at the right hand of God. Set your

3 Wuest's Word Studies, Volume 1, The Book of Romans by Kenneth Wuest, Grand Rapids, Michigan Wm. B. Eerdman's Publishing Company, (©1973), pp. 40-41.

mind on things above, not on things on the earth." If we want to live from heaven to earth, we need to think as Jesus thinks.

One of the practical ways to adapt to Jesus' thinking is to take every thought captive to Him. In 2 Corinthians 10:3-6 it says, "For though we walk in the flesh, we do not war according to the flesh. For the weapons of our warfare are not carnal but mighty in God for pulling down strongholds, casting down arguments and every high thing that exalts itself against the knowledge of God, bringing every thought into captivity to the obedience of Christ, and being ready to punish all disobedience when your obedience is fulfilled." If we do not take our thoughts captive, they will take us captive. Repentance involves changing the mind by taking our thoughts captive to Jesus and letting His thoughts fill our minds. It works!

God's Goodness Leads Us to Repent or Change Our Thinking

Romans 2:4, "Or do you despise the riches of His goodness, forbearance, and longsuffering, not knowing that the goodness of God leads you to repentance?"

As we begin to recognize the goodness of God and our lack of an inherent right to it (because we are imperfect), we must because of the very nature of His goodness, repent of our sins. Repenting means turning away from. We must turn away from the sin that has interfered with our intimate relationship with God, our Provider, Rock, Portion, Strong Tower and very Life. We do not earn, nor do we deserve, God's goodness. He offers it freely because He loves us dearly. Yes, you, my child. You are beautiful in His sight. He created you. He made you in His own image. How can you not be beautiful to Him?

Every parent believes his or her child is beautiful, because the love felt for this child overrides any objective view of features. This is how God sees us. His love is so great, so deep and so wide that He sees only the beauty of His creation. His love never fades, even when we are "naughty". He often grieves over our choices and behavior, but His love for us never ceases. What amazing goodness flows from the heart of the Father!

"'Repentance' is from the word *metanoia* and is literally defined as 'knowing after' (from *meta* meaning 'after' and *noeo* meaning 'to know'). It is a new knowledge, perception or understanding that comes to us 'after' our previous understanding. It is a change of mind."[4]

God is out to change our thinking. This is done by leading us to repent and change our minds. We go from our way to God's way.

What thoughts do you need to change? His goodness can lead you to repent...change your mind.

4 Sheets, Dutch, Praying for America, Regal Books © 2001, Ventura, CA, pg. 89.

My Way Not-So-Good Goodness	God's Way Goodness

CHAPTER THREE

Seeing the Goodness of God as Moses Did

Exodus 33:18,19, "And he said, 'Please show me Your glory.' Then He said, 'I will make all My goodness pass before you, and I will proclaim the name of the Lord before you. I will be gracious to whom I will be gracious, and I will have compassion on whom I will have compassion.'"

Goodness Precedes Glory

It is almost impossible to discuss God's goodness without climbing up Mt. Sinai and revisiting the time and place where Moses pleaded with heaven to allow him to see the face of God. Moses in the above passage is asking God to show him His glory. And the first thing God does is to cause all His goodness to pass before him. I believe that God desires His Church in this hour to have a revelation of His glory. But a precursor to receiving a revelation of His glory in its fullness is to have a revelation like Moses of all God's goodness passing before him. For the Church or an individual today to receive a revelation of His glory, we need a revelation of His goodness! Do you want God to show you His glory!? Be on the lookout for His goodness!

In the last 10 years, God has been showing me His goodness by causing it to pass before me constantly. He shows me how good He is and does good things for me. He is doing good things for people all around. God is so good!

He has reminded me how gracious and compassionate He has been to me through my family. My wife, Terry and her love for me are a demonstration of God's goodness. I love her profoundly. He has shown me His love through my children and my grandchildren. I love them all dearly. Now I am a grandpa or Papa as my grandchildren Hailey, Emma, Justus and Addison all call me. Papa! It is my favorite title in the entire universe! I love them so much! Being a grandparent causes the goodness of God to pass before me in a whole new way. Over and over through my family and my brothers and sisters in Christ He has shown me His goodness. *God is sooooo good!*

God's Goodness is Seen in Salvation

I have seen God's goodness through salvation pass by my family. I had the privilege of leading my grandmother to Jesus Christ over the phone when she was in her nineties. God's goodness has truly been amazing in my family when it comes to His saving grace. At 95 years of age, my grandfather was led to Christ by his son, my dad, who was not saved. My unsaved father led my unsaved grandfather to Christ right before my grandfather died! I used to have the mindset that an unsaved person could not lead an unsaved person to Christ; but God's goodness is really good! In Matthew 19:25,26 it says, "When His disciples heard it, they were greatly astonished, saying, 'Who then can be saved?' But Jesus looked at them and said to them, 'With men this is impossible, but with God all things are possible.'" God shifted my thinking that day. It seemed impossible, but with God all things are possible!

The story goes that, my father called to tell me my grandfather was dying and wondered if he should leave the Seattle area and go back to Appleton, Wisconsin to see him. I said, "It might be your last chance to see Grandpa. Go!" I asked him, "Would you do me a favor? Would you take this tract from Billy Graham entitled, 'Steps to Peace with God,' and read it to Grandpa for me and pray the prayer with him if he wants to do it?" I told him, "I would never ask you to do anything else for me, but please do this." A few days later, my dad called saying that Grandpa had died. My dad was crying and grieving the loss of his dad. I, at the appropriate time, asked if he had read the tract to Grandpa. He said he did and he had received Christ. Isn't God good?! Later my dad gave his heart to Christ and served Him until he died at 92 years of age.

See God's goodness come full circle in my family...my cousin wanted my grandfather and grandmother to give their lives to Christ; she sent them a book never read. In one of my darkest hours I found the book, read it at my grandparent's home and was saved. Then, years later, I initiated my unsaved father in bringing Grandpa to Christ; and was privileged to lead my grandmother to the Lord also. God's goodness is really good!

God's Goodness is Seen in Healing

Our church family has been a witness of God's goodness; God has been healing people in our church, Sonrise Christian Center (formerly Sonrise Chapel). It is so good to see sick people healed. God is showing His goodness by saving people and delivering people.

It is priceless to see the joy on people's faces when they or one of their loved ones have been healed, saved or delivered. In Acts 10:38 it says, "How God anointed Jesus of Nazareth with the Holy Spirit and with power, who went about doing good and healing all who were oppressed by the devil, for God was with Him."

One of the ways God shows His goodness to people is by Jesus healing those who are oppressed by the devil. One of the "GOOD" things God has done in our church was to heal a lady from a rotted kidney and bladder, lupus and many other related diseases. It is amazing how God has done a creative miracle within her body. Today she is free!

At Sonrise Christian Center we have seen people healed from cancer, lupus, scoliosis, migraines, herniated discs, paralysis and many more things. Jesus in His goodness heals, delivers and glorifies the Father. God is so good that He loves to minister to people's needs. Matthew 9:35-38 says, "Then Jesus went about all the cities and villages, teaching in their synagogues, preaching the gospel of the kingdom, and healing every sickness and every disease among the people. But when He saw the multitudes, He was moved with compassion for them, because they were weary and scattered, like sheep having no shepherd. Then He said to His disciples, 'The harvest truly is plentiful, but the laborers are few. Therefore pray the Lord of the harvest to send out laborers into His harvest.'"

God the Father and Jesus love to minister to people in their need. Are you believing for unsaved people in your life to come to the Lord? Are you contending for healing either in yourself or a loved one?

One thing that has helped me see the goodness of God pass by me is looking at Scriptures on God's goodness. Let His Goodness pass before you as you read these passages:

Psalm 31:19, "Oh, how great is Your goodness, which You have laid up for those who fear You, which You have prepared for those who trust in You in the presence of the sons of men!"

Psalm 52:1, "Why do you boast in evil, O mighty man? The goodness of God endures continually."

2 Thessalonians 1:11, "Therefore we also pray always for you that our God would count you worthy of this calling, and fulfill all the good pleasure of His goodness and the work of faith with power."

Psalm 25:7, "Do not remember the sins of my youth, nor my transgressions; according to Your mercy remember me, for Your goodness' sake, O Lord."

2 Chronicles 6:41, "Now therefore, Arise, O Lord God, to Your resting place, You and the ark of Your strength. Let Your priests, O Lord God, be clothed with salvation, and let Your saints rejoice in goodness."

Nehemiah 9:25, "And they took strong cities and a rich land, and possessed houses full of all goods, cistern already dug, vineyards, olive groves, and fruit trees in abundance. So they ate and were filled and grew fat, and delighted themselves in Your great goodness."

1 Chronicles 17:26, "And now, Lord, You are God, and have promised this goodness to Your servant."

Acts 14:17, "Neverless He did not leave Himself without witness, in that He did good, gave us rain from heaven and fruitful seasons, filling our hearts with food and gladness."

Psalm 107:8, "Oh, that men would give thanks to the Lord for His goodness, and for His wonderful works to the children of men!"

Psalm 86:5, "For You, Lord, are good, and ready to forgive, and abundant in mercy to all those who call upon You."

Psalm 119:68, "You are good, and do good; teach me Your statutes."

Psalm 107:9, "For He satisfies the longing soul, and fills the hungry soul with goodness."

Nahum 1:7, "The Lord is good, a stronghold in the day of trouble; and He knows those who trust in Him."

Jeremiah 31:14, "I will satiate the soul of the priests with abundance, and My people shall be satisfied with My goodness, says the Lord."

Jeremiah 31:12, "Therefore they shall come and sing in the height of Zion, streaming to the goodness of the Lord – for wheat and new wine and oil, for the young of the flock and the herd; their souls shall be like a well-watered garden, and they shall sorrow no more at all."

Mediate on these verses. Ask God to reveal His goodness to you in a new and powerful way!

Let God's goodness pass before your eyes; be on the lookout for it. When you see it, you can receive it!

Reflect and Discuss

What stands out to you in these verses?

How is God's goodness passing by you?

Declare His goodness over your life and into your situations.

CHAPTER FOUR

Seeing the Goodness of God in Creation

Genesis 1:31, "Then God saw everything that He had made, and indeed it was very good. So the evening and the morning were the sixth day."

It is impossible to fully comprehend the goodness of God. We think we know, but in truth we simply have no capability to appreciate everything He has done for us. We try to understand His goodness in worldly terms like the way we treat other people, how they repay our good deeds and so on and so forth. This becomes our model, our standard of measure on how to grasp the complete meaning of goodness. Yet this is an imperfect method because as you know we are flawed individuals, our righteousness is nothing compared to God. We are limited in what we can do, we can only help a few and we can only give according to our meager resources. Therefore, we can only guesstimate what it truly means to be good and how to do good. Our Father-God on the other hand can draw out blessing upon blessing from an inexhaustible supply. And most important of all, He is good to us according to a standard that is entirely His own (Isaiah 55:9).

Although we are now convinced that we cannot fathom the depths of His goodness, we are at the same time aware of Father-

God's great effort to teach us about His goodness. Our first stop is in the Book of Genesis wherein God created perfection and beauty out of an inherent goodness that is beyond words to describe. This is because the goodness of God is not simply a character trait. His goodness is actually part of His nature. It is more than an attribute. It is not just one of God's names but a major part of His nature.

God is not good because He exhibits the characteristic of a nice, kind, gentle, generous and loving deity. God is good because that is a major part of His core nature. Jesus, the only begotten of the triune Godhead said it best, "…No one is good – except God alone" (Luke 18:19, NIV). Jesus is privy to a revelation, which we are not, but we will try to find out what He knew by investigating where He has been and what He was doing there. We will not go only to the Gospels to see Jesus in human form. We need to go back much further – to the beginning of time.

In Psalm 33:5 God says, "He loves righteousness and justice; the earth is full of the goodness of the Lord." Everywhere we look in the earth we can see the good will of the Lord. Look at the sky, the stars, the mountains, the rivers, the spheres, the lakes, the sunrise in Uganda, all remind us of His goodness. There are so many beautiful sights that we see every day demonstrating that the earth is filled with the goodness of God.

The Goodness of God Partially Revealed in the Creation Process

The Bible tells us that Jesus was present in the day of creation. Let us revisit that event and try to discern as Jesus did. The creation account is found in the Book of Genesis. It is important to note that the story of beginnings started in the dark, formless and empty world. It was the author's way of saying that it started from nothing. And yet when God came near, all of a sudden the vacuum of space came alive with matter and living things. These are not the byproduct of the cosmic blunder but the result of a deliberate act by the Trinity. The Father-God verbally made known His desires; the Holy Spirit was hovering over the darkness as He enforced the will of the Father and Jesus did some of the heavy lifting- as usual- as He obeyed the Father like a dutiful Son. And so Jesus was honored with this affirmation, "Through him all things were made; without him nothing was made that has been made. In him was life, and that life was the light of all mankind" (John 1:3-4, NIV).

When the command was issued, "Let there be light," the Triune Godhead worked in perfect unison to create light. The same thing can be said when they created water, land, flowers, trees, birds, cattle and wild animals. Jesus was in the midst of the creation process, working hand-in-hand with the Father and the Holy Spirit. Jesus came to earth in the form of human flesh, and when He was given the opportunity to describe God, He said God is good. Jesus' statement is supported in the creation account because God took a break from designing, perfecting and ordering the universe; He surveyed His handiwork and this was the verdict He gave according to the scriptures: "God saw all that He had made, and it was very good."

God is the magnificent Creator. In Genesis 1:31, "Then God saw everything that He had made, and indeed it was very good. So the evening and the morning were the sixth day." In order to understand the last statement, you have to remind yourself that when God initiated the creation process He started with nothing. He was like a painter facing a blank canvas or a writer given a blank sheet of paper. If the painter is trained in realism, then he will paint a picture so lifelike the image may seem to jump out of the frame. If the painter is trained in abstract art, then he would create a masterpiece with beautiful images that are difficult to comprehend. If the writer is fluent in French, then he will produce French prose. If the writer is inspired, then the words that he will type on the blank screen will lift up the spirit of the reader. In other words God can only produce something that is inherent in Him.

It will help you further by realizing that unlike the artist and writer, God had to create His own paint, keyboard, brush and His own paper. This is why the created world is a true reflection of God's nature. Everything you see in the natural world comes from somewhere deep within God's inner being. When given the opportunity to describe the by-product of His core-nature, God said that it was very good (Genesis 1:31). It was very good indeed. We see the reflection of the Creator in all of creation, especially when you look at man and woman, the duo created in His image.

Reflecting on the animals God has created, we see how beautiful and good they are in His eyes. *How good to see this.* One of my favorite animals is an eagle. I love to see the magnificence of the eagle's flight. He soars on the winds. God wants us to soar like eagles in His goodness. Isaiah 40:31, "But those who wait on the Lord shall renew their strength; they shall mount up with wings like eagles, they shall run and not be weary, they shall walk and not faint." The eagle, created for His glory, reflects His goodness.

The deer, so graceful and strong, is another one of my favorite animals. It is fun to watch them run and jump through the woods. Psalm 42:1,2 it says, "As the deer pants for the water brooks, so pants my soul for You, O God. My soul thirsts for God, for the living God. When shall I come and appear before God?" In this metaphor, God tells of the deer panting after water when it is thirsty, it goes to its source of water to quench that thirst. God is the giver of the living water, which we need!

Revelation 5:13 tells us about the creatures that are in the sea, "And every creature which is in heaven and on the earth and under the earth and such as are in the sea, and all that are in them, I heard saying: 'Blessing and honor and glory and power be to Him who sits on the throne, and to the Lamb, forever and ever!'" Some of my favorite animals are found in the water. I love dolphins, killer whales, salmon and the like. There is nothing quite like scuba diving in Maui, seeing all the different sea creatures and their brilliant colors and saying, "Wow, God, you are so creative!" The creatures in the sea declare blessing, honor, glory and power.

I have seen lions, leopards, giraffes, elephants, crocodiles and many other wild animals. They all illustrate the goodness of God. The earth is full of the goodness of God...we need simply to open our eyes and see it! In Psalm 24:1, *"The earth is the Lord's, and all its fullness, the world and those who dwell therein."* He desires His goodness to be seen by all of His creation.

Have you ever wondered why God bothered to create this planet? Surely there is a reason why He went through all the trouble of creating a well-ordered universe and a perfectly beautiful planet earth. The answer can be seen when analyzing the creation process. We see that at the end of that cycle, God had saved the best for last. In the finale, the Triune Godhead spoke out, "…Let us make mankind in our image, in our likeness, so that they may rule over the fish in the sea and the birds of the sky, over the livestock and all the wild animals, and over all the creatures that move along the ground" (Genesis 1:26, NIV). It turned out everything was a special gift for you and me.

God made gigantic trees, massive rock formations, sparkling waters, raging waterfalls, rampaging herds, fluffy clouds, mesmerizing gemstones, refreshing wind, soft earth, fragrant blooms, rest inducing greenery, tasty honey, relaxing sand, gentle waves and colorful sea creatures, not to keep it for Himself but to give it to mankind as a present. God did that to initiate a formal introduction. The Person in love with the human race has to reveal His true intentions and He chose to introduce Himself by the way of an extravagant gift. He wants us to know that He is good. His core nature is all about goodness. As we look deep into His eyes we will see that His goodness is the summation of His awesome power, kindness, generosity, wisdom and majesty. It was revealed through His creation. Now, leave your room, go out of the house, look around and you will see.

God's love is a major component to understand His goodness. I admit that we are barely scratching the surface when it comes to the revelation of God's goodness. But we will continue to dig deeper. However, this is just part of the whole package. We know this because this is what the Lord said to Moses, "…you cannot see my face, for no one may see me and live" (Exodus 33:20, NIV). Those who stare directly into the face of the Lord will surely die; not because He is a vengeful God; it is simply the consequences of frail human bodies unable to contain His power.

God's goodness is the aggregate of His many attributes such as love, power, wisdom, beauty and majesty. Let us go back to the creation narrative and there we will know for sure that the created things are mere reflections of God's core nature – the byproduct of His goodness. We will achieve this by highlighting some of the major creation moments and the resulting physical representation of God's glory:

Water – God's life-giving power – Psalm 1:3

Land – God's dependability – Isaiah 54:10

Flowers – God's beauty – Matthew 6:28,29

Trees – God's provision – Psalm 104:16

Birds – God's majesty – Proverbs 30:19

Wild animals – God's strength – Job 41:1-9; Genesis 49:9

Man and Woman – God's love – John 3:16

The Lord has created so much more. Even as we limit our discussion to these few topics we are already overwhelmed by the glory of God. The seven created things discussed here are distinct from each other. They are the expression of God's power, wisdom, beauty and majesty.

As we look into the created universe we cannot help but be amazed at God's goodness displayed in every creature and natural object. If God is only about power then He could have created a barren world and all the living things in it existed in dread, darkness and slavery. If God could have simply waved His hand and created a world that was barely habitable, would we still be obliged to worship Him? No one could go against Him because of His omnipotence and omniscience. However, we can say without reservation the phrase: Praise be to God; for He did not create a barely habitable earth, instead He created paradise. Were it not for our sins, this planet and all the living and non-living things that it contained could be discerned correctly as a conveyor and reflector of God's goodness.

Take for instance water. God could have made it a hastily assembled substance that is unstable and unreliable, yet water is the most dependable compound known to man. In pure form it is clear and desirable as a means to quench our thirst. It is able to dissolve minerals and at the same time well designed to absorb heat. This is why it is perfect as a means to carry nutrients and everything needed to sustain our body. This is also the reason why water is synonymous with life.

God revealed His goodness not only in creating water but also when He created its counterpart, which is land. When God made land He made sure that it would sustain life. It provides not only a means to anchor fruit trees but also is a stable platform that allows human beings to walk and build their dwelling places. Aside from that, soil is a fascinating material. When a plant or animal dies it breaks down and its simpler components are absorbed into the soil. Thus, the soil is not only a means to which plants and fruit trees cling, but it also helps to facilitate the intake of water and minerals and is a major component of the living and breathing plant.

God could have created a world impossible to maintain. If He did not create water and land to interact this way, then dead animals and rotten plant matter would fall to the ground and decay ever so slowly. The putrid smell would envelop the atmosphere and the earth would have been a place of torment. By creating a systematic environment the Lord displayed His spectacular wisdom and demonstrated that goodness penetrates His being.

Let us invite Jesus in for a moment and request Him to give a short commentary regarding flowering plants, the next major creative thing on the list. And this is what He said, "...*See how the flowers of the field grow. They do not labor or spin. Yet I tell you that not even Solomon in all his splendor was dressed like one of these*" (Matthew 6:28,29, NIV). It is amazing to hear it straight from the Source. We were made to realize that God could have decided to create an ugly planet. There is nothing we could have done about it except to endure that incessant suffering that would have resulted from a mean-spirited decision. However, our Lord is good.

Jesus added that it was God's decision to clothe the flowers of field with such extravagance even if their lifespan will never last for more than a few days (Matthew 6:30). Let us be awed by such level of generosity. Furthermore, let us come to understand that the Lord cannot give what He did not posess in the first place. It would have been impossible for Him to clothe flowers with finery if He Himself were not filled to overflowing with beauty. God's astounding splendor is part of His goodness and it is in full display in creation.

A forest full of trees, birds and wild animals is a testimony to God's sustaining grace. Winter, spring, summer and fall; no matter what the season, the ecosystem that God has created will remain the same. It is renewed on a daily basis demonstrating the Lord's power, wisdom, beauty and splendor but also His faithfulness. We are sure that He is always there for us. There is no truth to the accusation that the moment God created the universe He turned around and abandoned His created worlds. In the perfection in the order of the planets, stars and galaxies we were given a pledge that He is watching over us. All of creation declares God's goodness. We will see the breath of His word reflected in His creation.

Reflect and Discuss

What parts of creation reminds you of the goodness of God?

CHAPTER FIVE

Seeing the Goodness of God Following Us

Psalm 23:6, "Surely goodness and mercy shall follow me all the days of my life; and I will dwell in the house of the Lord."

Psalm 23 is one of the most incredible passages in the Bible. It has been well loved by many throughout the ages. It has captured and comforted the hearts of many. It has always been special to me because it was my mother's favorite. She is buried at Evergreen Washelli Cemetery in Seattle, Washington. She died in a tragic automobile accident while on her way to help the first African-American woman, Lillian Boot, who moved into our community. Some angry, hate-filled person had set fire to her home and my mother died while making an effort to right a wrong. Lillian was a precious Christian woman who loved the Lord.

Many years after my mother died, God's goodness was poured on me. Lillian showed up at the church I pastor and asked to honor my mother and I. Lillian told my church family that my mother had laid down her life for her. Quoting Jesus she said, *"Greater love has no one than this, than to lay down one's life for his friends"* (John 15:13). God cares about everything that concerns us. 1 Peter 5:7 says, *"Casting all your care upon*

Him, for He cares for you." He is a Good Shepherd...a great Shepherd...THE CHIEF SHEPHERD!

I have witnessed as I pursue God, a sense of something sneaking up behind me and following me. It is His goodness and mercy! Every day of my life, if I look over my shoulder, I see it again...yes...His goodness and mercy following me. We will not only live in the house of the Lord forever and ever, but in this life we will surely see His goodness and mercy following us.

God's Goodness in Real Life!

The more I look for His goodness in life and in the Scriptures, the more I see it everywhere. The devil and the world want us to only see the evil that is around us. The newspapers, Internet and television surround us with it; but when we put on God's goodness glasses we begin to see what He is doing in the world.

In one 24-hour period, God granted me a couple of the desires of my heart. My wife, some friends and I were taken on a trip to Israel by Jane Hansen Hoyt, President of Aglow International. Someone paid for our entire trip! I was overwhelmed, I cried with joy, thanking the Father, Jesus the Son and the Holy Spirit for their incredible goodness. The other desire was the opportunity to read the biography of Derek Prince by Stephen Mansfield. It seemed such a little and frivolous request to ask God compared to the other things He had already done!

One day not long after, Marty Evans, one of our deacons, appeared at my front door holding a brown paper bag. (I'd had the privilege of leading Marty and his wife Nancy to Christ.) Marty told me that after volunteering at a Chuck Pierce conference, he was offered some free books from the bookstore. He'd felt a strong urging from the Holy Spirit to give a particular book to me. Lo and behold, the book in his bag was the biography of Derek Prince I'd told God I was longing to read. Marty must have thought something was terribly wrong when I began crying, but I was finally able to explain that I was weeping because of God's goodness to me. I shared with him some of the wonderful ways I'd been seeing and receiving His goodness. This was just one more very personal wonder!

Goodness from the Good Shepherd

We must acknowledge that our God is Lord. He is owner of everything that we have including the very breath that we take in every second of the day. The moment we no longer struggle with that idea it becomes easier for us to be under His authority and influence. When we are already in His Kingdom then we are entitled to whatever privileges are available to the citizens of that realm.

God's goodness surrounds us. He holds us in the palm of His hand, but He also holds His arms beneath us so if we fall He can catch us. He will fight off our enemy if we turn to Him in time of trouble. In Psalm 46:1-3 it says, "God is our refuge and strength, a very present help in trouble. Therefore we will not fear, even though the earth be removed, and though the mountains be carried into the midst of the sea; thought its waters roar and be trouble, though the mountains shake with it swelling. Selah."

In Romans 8:32, "He who did not spare His own Son, but delivered Him up for us all, how shall He not with Him also freely give us all things?" God is so good He cares about every big and little thing in your life. Watch out…His goodness and mercy are sneaking up behind you and following you every day! If you do not believe me, look over your shoulder!

The central message of Psalm 23 is our God is a Good Shepherd. If we belong to Him, and if He is in us, His goodness will follow us all the days of our human existence. Jesus validated David's Psalm when He came to earth and said, "I am the good shepherd" (John 10:11).

We often do not think we deserve the goodness of God. The good news is that we do not get what we deserve; we get what Jesus deserves!

God's Goodness and Favor Surround Us

God's goodness and favor go hand in hand. We can be a Christian for all of our lives but never be able to gain access to this level of God's supernatural favor and goodness. Nevertheless, we know that this is open for all simply because it was written in the Bible. If God's supernatural favor and goodness was merely a personal transaction between David and God, then we can forget about it all. But we know that an invitation to experience a deeper life in God has been given a long time ago. It is a gift extended to all humanity.

The Psalms of David are full of prophetic promises about God's goodness and favor. Not only does God's goodness surround you, but His favor surrounds you! In Psalm 5:12, "For You, O Lord, will bless the righteous; with favor You will surround him as with a shield." God loves to bless the righteous with favor. How does He surround us with His favor and goodness?

As we look into God's Word, we see how He surrounds us. Psalm 32:7-9 says, "You are my hiding place; You shall preserve me from trouble; You shall surround me with songs of deliverance. Selah. I will instruct you and teach you in the way you should go; I will guide you with My eye. Do not be like the horse or like the mule, which have no understanding, which must be harnessed with a bit and bridle, else they will not come near you." God surrounds us with the songs of deliverance. Many times when I hear Christian songs they become my songs of deliverance. God also instructs us with His eyes and shows the way we should go in life. The Psalmist David uses the horse and the mule as examples: the mule tends to be stubborn and the bit and bridle are used to move him. The horse tends to want to run ahead without restraint and the bit and bridle harnesses his strength. So don't be like a mule stubborn and resistant where God will have to "pull you." Do not be like the horse who runs ahead of God – or He will restrain you. You are surrounded by His goodness and favor.

The reason God's goodness and mercy follow you every day of your life is because the Lord Himself surrounds you.

Psalm 125:2, "As the mountains surround Jerusalem, so the Lord surrounds His people from this time forth and forever." This Psalm tells us we can trust God! If we trust, we are like Mount Zion – we will not be moved. God will protect you on all sides. God's goodness and mercy surround you everywhere you go each day.

Reflect and Discuss

How have you seen His goodness and mercy follow you?

How has God surrounded you?

CHAPTER SIX

Seeing the Goodness of God Ahead in Hope

Psalm 27:13-14, "I would have lost heart, unless I had believed that I would see the goodness of the Lord in the land of the living. Wait on the Lord; be of good courage, and He shall strengthen your heart; wait, I say, on the Lord!"

The Psalmist David wrote Psalm 27. The Psalm is full of declarations of David's faith in God. I love it! He declares, "The Lord is my light and my salvation; whom shall I fear?" (verse 1). He tells how God will protect him in verse 3, "Though an army may encamp against me, my heart shall not fear; though war may rise against me, in this I will be confident." In verse 14, "Wait on the Lord; be of good courage, and He shall strengthen your heart; wait, I say, on the Lord!" While we are waiting to see the goodness of the Lord in the land of the living we can wait on Him. As we wait on Him in good courage He strengthens our heart.

You might be in a difficult situation with your child, spouse, job, relationship, financial difficulty and or any circumstance. You can trust God. Hebrews 6:12 says, "That you do not become sluggish, but imitate those who through faith and patience inherit the promises." You will see the goodness of God in the land of the living! Remember that God's promises are not dependent on the circumstances, but on His ability to perform them. Sometimes there is a timing issue, or He is developing His character in our lives. Keep waiting! Joseph was willing to wait many years until his dream became a reality. It took 25 years for Abraham to have the character to be a father of many nations. You will see the goodness of God in the land of living!

The devil wants to discourage us. He wants to take our courage out of us. God wants to encourage us. He wants to put courage in us! God wants to put courage in you today! In Psalm 27:14, David, under the Holy Spirit's inspiration wrote, "Wait on the Lord…"

Wait on the Lord

In verse 13, David states, *"I would have lost heart, <u>unless</u> I had believed that I would <u>see</u> the goodness of the Lord in the land of the living"* (emphases mine). In the middle of the struggles you and I can believe to see the goodness of the Lord. It will show up on the radar screen, so keep looking and believing. The enemy wants you to faint and lose heart. Faith in God's goodness strengthens our hearts. If we believe we will see it…I'm talking about God's goodness in the land of the living! When you are overwhelmed, keep on hoping, praying and waiting. Keep your eyes on God and His goodness.

Faith is the Key

Believing is the key to seeing God's goodness in the land of the living. In Romans 10:17, "So, then faith comes by hearing, and hearing by the word of God." Ephesians 6:16 says, "Above all, taking the shield of faith with which you will be able to quench all the fiery darts of the wicked one." God can help our faith in the midst of our battles. "The word 'quench' in this verse is the Greek word sbennumi, which means to quench by dousing or to extinguish by drowning in water. It refers to the water-soaked shield of Roman soldiers. You see, before Roman soldiers went out to battle, they purposely soaked their shields in water until they were completely water-saturated. The soldiers did this because they knew the enemy would be shooting fire-bearing arrows in their direction. If a shield was dry, it was possible for it to be set it on fire when struck. But, if this vital piece of armor was water-soaked, the flames would be extinguished even if an arrow penetrated its heavily saturated surface."[5] The faith that comes from hearing the Word of God is likened to a water-saturated shield. As we stand and believe for victory through the scriptures they repel the devil's fiery darts.

If we continue to do good and obey God in the midst of the battle, we will see God's goodness. Galatians 6:9 says, "And let us not grow weary while doing good, for in due season we shall reap if we do not lose heart." Continually walk in faith and do not give up! The devil will tell you to lose heart, but you do not have to. Keep enduring in the battle and you will wear out the devil. The "word 'faint' comes from the Greek word ekluo, which means to loosen up; to relax; to faint; and to lose altogether. The devil will say, 'This doesn't work. You've tried long enough. It won't hurt if you cut back on your giving. Loosen up a little. Relax from giving so much."[6] Keep planting the seeds of God's Word in your heart and water them daily.

Another key to receiving God's promise is faith mixed with patience. In Hebrews 10:36 it says, "For you have need of endurance, so that after you have done the will of God, you may receive the promise." Faith and patience or endurance help us see God's goodness in the land of the living. Staying true to the promises in the midst of difficult circumstances helps us obtain the power. Stay strong in faith and watch God show up. Do the will of God and you will receive the promise. Stand strong! Stand firm! Stand in faith! Stand in patience! The book of Hebrews in Chapter 11 is full of faith examples. Hebrews 11:6 says, "But without faith it is impossible to please Him, for he who comes to God must believe that He is, and that He is a rewarder of those who diligently seek Him." God will reward your faith and patience.

---

5 Renner, Rick, Sparkling Gems from the Greek, Tulsa, OK, © 2003, pg. 659.

6 Ibid, pg. 557.

Reflect and Discuss

Has God promised you something that you are waiting for? Explain.

Don't lose heart. Keep your eyes on the Promiser and His promises.

SECTION TWO
Receiving His Goodness

RECEIVING GOODNESS THROUGH TASTING IT
RECEIVING THE FRUIT OF THE SPIRIT
DELIGHTING IN THE GOODNESS OF GOD

Psalm 34:8, "Oh, taste and see that the Lord is good; blessed is the man who trusts in Him!"

The Psalmist David wrote Psalm 34 when he pretended madness before Abimilech, who drove him away. What an interesting experience to say, *"Oh, taste and see that the Lord is good..."* We all love to eat and have our favorite foods. In this Psalm, David uses an analogy of tasting God to describe how he received God's goodness. It's great to smell food, but it's certainly a lot better to taste it! As you and I swallow food, we ingest it and savor its good taste.

The longer I know the Lord in my life the hungrier I am for His presence. He is the only one who can satisfy the deep longing of my soul and spirit. In Exodus 33:14 God said to Moses, "My Presence will go with you, and I will give you rest." After we have eaten a great meal, we are satisfied and at rest. The word "give rest" in the Hebrews is "nu'ach, to rest, settle down; to be soothed or quieted; to be secure; to be still; to dwell peacefully. In the present reference, God's presence soothes, comforts, settles, consoles and quiets us."[7] When we taste and receive God's goodness, it soothes, comforts and settles us.

In 1 Peter 2:3, "If indeed you have tasted that the Lord is gracious." When we taste of the Lord's love, you know how gracious He is to us. In the context of 1 Peter 2, he is talking about newborn babies desiring the pure milk of the Word. The Word is what new believers need to be fed so they may grow. Taste and see the Lord is good and gracious.

---

7 The New Spirit-filled Bible, Jack Hayford, Executive Editor, Thomas Nelson Bibles, © 2002, Nashville, TN, pg. 120.

CHAPTER SEVEN

Receiving the Goodness of God Through Tasting it

What is even more wonderful is when we know Jesus Christ as our Lord and Savior. We will never have to taste eternal death; we have partaken or tasted eternal life. In John 8:52, the Jews said to Jesus, "...Now we know that You have a demon! Abraham is dead, and the prophets; and You said, 'If anyone keeps My word he shall never taste death.'" All I used to taste before I gave my life to Jesus Christ was death. But now that I know Him, I taste His life! The word taste in John 8:52 in the Hebrew geuomai which means "to eat, partake of, feel, experience. Geuomai is used both naturally and metaphorically, especially to describe the personal experience of death, whether Christ's (Hebrews 2:9) or the believer's (Matthew 16:28, John 8:52)."[8] You can eat, partake of, feel and experience the life of God when Christ is your Lord in this world and in the world to come.

Taste His Presence

In Exodus 33:15 Moses said to God, "...If Your Presence does not go with us, do not bring us up from here." In verse 17 of this passage, the Lord says, "...for you have found grace in My

---

8 Ibid., pg. 1459.

sight, and I know you by name." God was saying to Moses, "I am pleased with you." Why was God pleased with Moses and why did He grant his request? Moses realized that whether he was in the Desert of Sinai or the Promised Land flowing with milk and honey, there was not much difference without His presence.

The presence of God makes your home His home. The presence of God in a nation can bless it. Our body is the temple of the Holy Spirit – we carry the presence of God. Psalm 16:11, "You will show me the path of life; in Your presence is fullness of joy; at Your right hand are pleasures forevermore." Oh, taste and see that the Lord is good! If you are hungry and thirsty for His presence, He will fill you up and fill you to overflowing! David, remembering God allowed him to escape from Abimilech, wrote about tasting the Lord.

The Psalmist could not contain his excitement when he discovered the benefits of knowing God and so he said, "Taste and see that the Lord is good" (Psalm 34:8). There are so many things that we can glean from this statement. First, there is absolutely no struggle the moment we decide to take the leap and dive into the presence of God. It is as easy as eating a meal. Second, there is an absolute guarantee that you will be satisfied. It is like going into a five-star restaurant, you know that you will get something out of that experience. The only difference with God is that you eat free. And finally, we are told God is easily accessible and so we get to know Him 24 hours a day, seven days a week. We had been told how excellent is the goodness of God and we had been given a free invitation to feast in God's house. So what are we waiting for? Let us come and enter in.

In Psalm 34 David used the analogy of tasting food to describe how he discovered God's goodness. There is a reason why he chose to illustrate his experience this way. As we all know we cannot partake of a meal if we are not invited to join in. We cannot eat if we are not welcomed to enter the house and then allowed to sit in the dining room to enjoy the food. We cannot eat unless we are near the food. And finally, we can enjoy the food when it is swallowed, ingested and then savor its good taste.

The same can be said about the feasting in the presence of God. He has to send the formal invitation first before we can enter the house of the Lord (Psalm 122). He has to take the initiative to invite us so that we can be filled with the Holy Spirit. And when we are aware that such an invitation does exist, we must not delay but receive it with all our hearts. In this manner the presence of God will be upon us and we will experience life to the fullest (1 Samuel 16:13).

Hidden From His Presence

We may have access to knowledge, power and wealth and yet if we don't have access to the presence of God, all of these things will give us sorrow instead of joy. We have to make sure that His presence is with us all the days of our lives. There is a story in the Book of Genesis that perfectly illustrates the tragic consequences that can happen when cut off from the presence of God. The story involves the first son of Adam. Initially he brought joy to the lives of Adam and Eve since he was the firstborn. However, Cain was a hot-tempered man and he was not submissive to God's will over his life. One day, in blinding rage he struck and killed his brother. What transpired next is a picture of how a curse, instead of blessing, can descend upon a person. The main reason many people struggle in this lifetime can be illustrated through the conversation between God and Cain (Genesis 4:10-14):

"And He said, 'What have you done? The voice of your brother's blood cries out to Me from the ground. So now you are cursed from the earth, which has opened its mouth to receive your brother's blood from your hand. When you till the ground, it shall no longer yield its strength to you. A fugitive and a vagabond you shall be on the earth.' And Cain said to the Lord, 'My punishment is greater than I can bear! Surely You have driven me out this day from the face of the ground; I shall be hidden from Your face; I shall be a fugitive and a vagabond on the earth, and it will happen that anyone who finds me will kill me.'"

The Lord revealed to Cain the consequence for his wicked behavior and began to show him that he would experience a hard life and become a restless wanderer on the earth. Cain acknowledged that he will reap what he had sown and capped it off by identifying the real reason why problems are piling up and he said, "…I will be hidden from your presence" (Genesis 4:14, NIV).

Notice that Cain will always be visible to God. It is Cain who can no longer see and feel the presence of God. It is this disability that hampers his capability to access the goodness of the Lord. There are two key words in this passage that best described the impact of being cut off from God's presence and these are restlessness and homelessness. The accursed person ultimately becomes a restless wanderer. We can call this the "Curse of Cain."

This special type of curse spread through the whole earth like a plague. It does not require a special kind of sin in order to be stung by its venom. We only have to be cut-off from God's presence. If we are hidden from the presence of God then we walk this planet like a living dead man. We are restless due to a deep-seated discontent that is impossible to define, and bewildered by a sense of hunger that we are powerless to satisfy. Our minds and inner being cannot focus on one task, and we look with envy to places that seem to have greener pastures and so we jump from place to place. We are forced to go through this futile process because we don't have a true spiritual home.

Two famous heroes of the faith who experienced what it means to have the "Curse of Cain" were Jacob, one of the patriarchs of Israel, and his great grandson, Moses, also known as the Prince of Egypt. In each case, sin forced them to run away but ultimately they suffered because of their inability to access what their fathers enjoyed even when they were sojourners in a foreign land. Jacob fell in love with deceitfulness and guile, so he was driven out of his home. He became a spiritual nomad and it took him more than 14 years to obtain the rest needed by his mind, body and soul. He received this blessing when he met God at a riverbank and only after Jacob embraced Him fiercely like a wrestler forcing something out of his foe. You can just imagine how much he must have regretted not cultivating a relationship with the Lord.

Moses was restless too. He wanted to free his people and tried to take matters into his own hands. As a result he killed an Egyptian, fled into the Midian wilderness and spent 40 years wandering as a shepherd developing his character. He experienced God's goodness at the burning bush in the wilderness and when he was ready, the Lord sent him to free his people. You will see the goodness of the Lord by tasting it!

Are you trying to hide something from God? Have you made a wrong turn when God told you to go another way? Have you sinned and are you running from God? His Goodness will chase you down.

Reflect and Discuss

How are you tasting the goodness of God?

Are you running away from God?

CHAPTER EIGHT

Receiving the Goodness of God – The Fruit of the Spirit

Galatians 5:22-23, "But the fruit of the Spirit is love, joy, peace, longsuffering, kindness, goodness, faithfulness, gentleness, self-control. Against such there is no law."

The fruit of the Spirit grows in our life as we cooperate with the Holy Spirit. As we allow Him to work in us, we are transformed. John Wesley said,

"Do all the good you can,

"By all the means you can,

"In all the ways you can,

"In all the places you can,

"At all the times you can,

"To all the people you can,

As long as ever you can."[9]

God's goodness is different from "good works" to gain merit. It springs forth from the indwelling Spirit. Paul says in Romans 15:14, "Now I myself am confident concerning you, my brethren,

---

9 Dean, Eleanor, *Speaker's Source*, Zondervan Publishing House, Grand Rapids, MI 1960, pg. 114.

that you also are full of goodness, filled with all knowledge, able also to admonish one another." We share God's goodness with one another. Our being good results in our doing good. Think of how you have received God's goodness through other people! God develops the fruit of the Spirit of goodness within us.

In Ephesians 5:8-10, Paul shares, "For you were once darkness, but now you are light in the Lord. Walk as children of light (for the fruit of the Spirit is in all goodness, righteousness, and truth), finding out what is acceptable to the Lord." In this context, Paul is teaching on light versus darkness. We should be walking opposite of the ways we did when we walked in darkness. As children of the light let His goodness shine through you! Goodness is acceptable in the sight of the Lord.

Acts 10:38, in speaking of Jesus it says, "How God anointed Jesus of Nazareth with the Holy Spirit and with power, who went about doing good and healing all who were oppressed by the devil, for God was with Him." Jesus' goodness attracted many to the Father and into the Kingdom. We can follow His example, do good and bring healing to those oppressed by the devil, because God is with us!

We Are His Workmanship

We have been planted in Christ and out of the outflow of His life develops the supernatural fruit of goodness in us. We cooperate with the Holy Spirit to cultivate the fruit of the Spirit in our lives. In Ephesians 2:10 it says, "For we are His workmanship, created in Christ Jesus for good works, which God prepared beforehand that we should walk in them." The word workmanship is poiema in the Greek language, which is poem or poetry, a work of an artisan. We are God's creative poetry and He has uniquely designed us to show forth good works. God's works flow out of a good heart. Matthew 12:35 says, "A good man out of the good treasure of his heart brings forth good things, and an evil man out of the evil treasure brings forth evil things." In its context it says that out of the abundance of the heart the mouth speaks. A good man - good heart - good things!

We usually equate the goodness of God with material blessings. This is understandable for this is simply human nature at work. We keep score by looking at our personal inventory and then we check the items on our list such as car, house, shirts, groceries, electronic gadgets, family vacations abroad, etc. Again, there is nothing wrong with this picture because the Lord is mindful of our needs and even desires to give us more than the basic necessities of life such as food, clothing and shelter. On the other hand, we have to ask, what if the real measure of God's goodness is not seen in the things that we can consume, but rather in the things that can be grown in the spirit?

What if the real inheritance that God wants us to covet are not land titles and precious metals? What if it is the fruit of the Spirit that grows deep within us? It is the secret to having an abundant life. It is defined as the ability to receive God's goodness and then share it with others. We have come to know the goodness of God but it must not be hoarded, it must be shared.

An abundant life does not consist of power, wealth and fame. It is defined rather by our ability to live in accordance with the will of God without experiencing any conflict of interest. This is a more complicated way of saying that we must be free from sin. An abundant life is also defined by an obedient heart willing to observe the commandments of the Lord. Furthermore, an abundant life is seen in the depth of our service to others, in how we are able to give without expecting anything in return. We must be free, we must learn to obey and we need to serve others because this is the essence of life.

We know so well how easily we are ensnared by the traps laid down by the enemy and the world. We also know how easy it is for us to disobey, turn our backs on God and continue with our wicked ways. We are in constant rebellion when it comes to God's directive to love our neighbors as ourselves, because we don't know how to express faith through love (Galatians 5:6). We need to live in accordance to freedom, obedience and service; however we can only do it if we prioritize the cultivation of the fruit of the Spirit rather than expend all our energies in the collection of material things that are here today and gone tomorrow.

What Does it Mean to Have an Abundant Life?

When Jesus summarized the main reason why He came down to earth, this is what He said, "...I have come that they may have life, and that they may have it more abundantly" (John 10:10, NIV). As we take a closer look at Jesus' words we will discover that this promise is a two-step process. First, He will give us life, and then He will make us experience life to the fullest.

There is a need to explain these words using two illustrations. Picture a gas stove. We turn it on by twisting the knob, we hear the click of the igniter and the spark it generates will produce fire. But it is only when we turn the knob counterclockwise that the stove can be made to produce a bluish hot flame and therefore allows us to cook great tasting food at high heat.

Now, imagine a sports car sitting in a garage. The owner gets in, turns on the ignition switch and in a split-second the engine roars to life. He will shift to the lowest gear, ease down the gas pedal to move the vehicle slowly. This is just the first phase though, because when the car is on the open road, there will be a shifting of gears, the gas pedal is pushed to the floor and the vehicle will accelerate to the exhilaration and satisfaction of the driver.

In these two illustrations we have seen how a "spark of life" started up a good thing. However, we must understand that is just prelude to something much better. We can enjoy life more if there is a way to move up to the next level, to allow the flames to burst into high heat and to speed up the car by revving it into high gear. We can only do so if we know how to get past the initial stage. There are so many believers in Christ who are content to lead a life of mediocrity while others, who want more out of life, make the mistake of going after worthless things. In these end times it has become increasingly clear that every believer's life must count; it is time to move up and desire life in abundance.

So now we have to stop and ask: What does it mean to live life to the fullest? Jesus gave a hint when He told His disciples about the parable of the rich fool. In this short tale Jesus talked about a rich landowner who had a bumper harvest that was so tremendous he had to build bigger barns to store everything. This means surplus money for the rich man and enabling him to acquire more stuff, fancier toys, more land, etc. But that night, after writing down his short-term and long-term plans he died in his sleep. In the introduction to this story Jesus issued a warning: "Take heed and beware of covetousness, for one's life does not consist in the abundance of the things he possesses" (Luke 12:15). Jesus made an emphatic statement that having an abundant life has nothing to do with money and the things that go with it. Therefore, an abundant life is accessible only through the spiritual and not the temporal.

Life in the Spirit Bears Fruit

For many of us our lives are defined by our possessions; however, Jesus' words are as clear as day: life does not consist in an abundance of possessions. We cannot be sustained, be made alive and reach our full potential – to live in accordance to our design and destiny if we are merely focused on our acquisitions. If an abundant life is only possible in the Lord then we must listen to His teachings and this is what He said: "It is the Spirit who gives life; the flesh profits nothing. The words that I speak to you are spirit, and they are life" (John 6:63).

When we listen to the words of Jesus we receive the "words of life" and become new citizens of His Kingdom. As we continue to press on and passionately persevere to learn more of Christ this is what is in store for us according to His Word:

"I am the true vine, and My Father is the vinedresser. Every branch in Me that does not bear fruit He takes away; and every branch that bears fruit He prunes, that it may bear more fruit. You are already clean because of the word which I have spoken to you. Abide in Me, and I in you. As the branch cannot bear fruit of itself, unless it abides in the vine, neither can you, unless you abide in Me. I am the vine, you are the branches. He who abides in Me, and I in him, bears much fruit; for without Me you can do nothing. If anyone does not abide in Me, he is cast out as a branch and is withered; and they gather them and throw them into the fire, and they are burned. If you abide in Me, and My words abide in you, you will ask what you desire, and it shall be done for you. By this My Father is glorified, that you bear much fruit; so you will be My disciples" (John 15:1-8).

When we listen and obey we become disciples of Christ and His Spirit dwells in us, we become fruitful beyond imagination. The Apostle Paul expounds this when he remarked, "But the fruit of the Spirit is love, joy, peace, longsuffering, kindness, goodness, faithfulness, gentleness, self-control. Against such there is no law" (Galatians 5:22,23). Upon reading this passage from Paul's letter to the Galatians everything becomes crystal clear. We can only have abundant life in Christ Jesus; as we abide in Him, the Holy Spirit will cause the reproduction of the fruit of the Spirit, which is actually the character of our Lord that He will graft into our inner-man.

This is the reason we become more than conquerors; the same reason why we can do everything through Christ our Lord, the same bedrock into which we stand and declare that we have life in abundance only if we are connected to the main Vine. In general terms, we can only sustain and even grow what we possess if we have the fruit of the Spirit within us. The fruit of the Spirit is a multifaceted gemstone and it will benefit us greatly if we can understand the value of each facet. The following is an attempt to focus the spotlight on this wonderful gift from above and thus understand why we are blessed if we bear this kind of fruit.

The fruit of the spirit allows us to live in harmony with the spirit, receive good things from above and then enjoy and keep them.

LOVE is at the heart of this fruit. Every good thing emanates from love. Everything is made possible because of God's love. We experience abundant life because we no longer see the world and everything it contains within the mindset of greed, hate and fear. Without love many are driven to accumulate wealth and never know when to stop and enjoy. We become like the rich man who spent every single moment of his life acquiring wealth and never had the chance to be of service to others. When he died his life had zero value; he did not live abundantly.

JOY is the byproduct of love. A burden is lifted from us when we no longer hate, are not fearful and are not anxious about what we will eat or what we will wear. We cannot do anything but be joyful. We rejoice because our souls delight in the contentment we receive from knowing that God absolutely loves us. Aside from that, we feel the joy of the Lord and it becomes our strength. This joy is infectious and it will spread in our workplace and community and as a result, our strength is multiplied. Thus we are able to accomplish much. Furthermore, joy increases our lifespan while worry and fear shorten it.

PEACE is the end result when a person's mind and heart are secure in the love of Father-God. When we know that there is someone who guards us and takes care of us as a Good Shepherd, then there is no reason to worry; we are at peace. The Apostle Paul exhorted the Philippians by writing, "And the peace of God, which surpasses all understanding, will guard your hearts and minds through Christ Jesus" (Philippians 4:7). But before that he told them to rejoice and he added, "Be anxious for nothing, but in everything by prayer and supplication, with thanksgiving, let your requests be made known to God" (Philippians 4:6). It is the same, as saying that if we are in the center of God's will then our prayers will be answered. Imagine what you can achieve when your whole being is at peace! Imagine the impact of a prayerful man or woman who knows how to receive good things from God.

PATIENCE is the end result of knowing that we have a prayer-answering God. It is an attitude that we cultivate when we walk in the Spirit, because as we deepen our intimacy with the Lord we will come to realize that He has plans to prosper us and not to harm us and that His ultimate goal is to give us a future (Jeremiah 29:11). This is a future living in a mansion with access roads paved in gold. If we have patience then we will not do crazy things that will endanger our lives. King Saul did not cultivate this fruit and so when he was in a bind he went ahead to solve his problem through his own strength and disobeyed God who told them to wait for His help (1 Samuel 15).

KINDNESS is the inevitable result if we know that there is nothing in this world that can separate us from God and His love. We can tolerate the abuses hurled at us because we have joy and peace in our hearts and minds. We can rest at ease in the presence of God who will guard us and make sure that tomorrow all our needs will be met. We don't need to compete and therefore we don't need to bare our fangs, sharpen our claws and fight it out with others in the marketplace, in our schools and community. We learn to develop a humble heart because we know that there is someone behind us who will ultimately give us victory in the things that really matter.

FAITHFULNESS is now easy to develop within our spirit. In the past we had no idea what it meant to be faithful. We thought that life was just a game you play and you must do everything to win it. The selfish attitude created in us a mindset that we can walk out of any relationship if it is no longer convenient. Thus, it is easy for many to leave their church, divorce spouses, abandon children and betray friendships for the sake of escaping the heat of trials and testing. But if we walk in the Spirit and hold onto relationships that are dear, we know that it is only by going through a purification process that we can begin to fully enjoy the benefits of these relationships. This also includes our relationship with God.

GENTLENESS has never been our strongest trait. We are not talking about being polite or observing social conventions. Gentleness is not just about being a gentleman or lady. There is more to it, for it is a combination of kindness, patience and humility. This is one of the major characteristics of Jesus and ironically enough it gave Him the power to do mighty things for God. The world has conditioned our minds to believe that being boisterous, arrogant and forceful is the only way to handle difficult situations. The Word of God teaches differently, because gentleness can open doors that previously were tightly shut. Gentleness is also like a fragrant spirit that attacks the broken, the oppressed and the marginalized. Thus, they will not hesitate to come near for help. As a result, we accomplish more if we are gentle than if we are not.

SELF-CONTROL is the end result if we are surrounded by God's love, joy, peace, patience, kindness, faithfulness and gentleness. We become like lambs assured of guidance and provisions under the care of the Good Shepherd. Contrast this to a person who does not have the fruit of the Spirit and you will find a man or a woman who indulges their sinful nature believing that each person is to his own, without regard to God and the community. Self-control is not a simple thing to God; without it we are prone to self-destructive behavior and its absence is oftentimes the cause of missed opportunities. We have seen it's destructive effect in the life of Achan, the son of Carmi (Joshua 7:1). He could not control himself and so he stole a portion of the war booty, which was consecrated to the Lord. He could not foresee that riches and glory were in store for Joshua's army; he thought about life in the moment and that he must seize the day. Ironically what little he had was even taken away from him, for his life was cut short.

GOODNESS is a facet of this gemstone that sparkles as beautifully as the others. It means that we can become the goodness of God on this earth. This is difficult to fathom; it is hard to believe that God is immensely gracious to us. He chose us to be His vessels of goodness so that the whole earth will be blessed through the works of His people (Genesis 12). Abundant life therefore does not consist in accumulated wealth but in serving God and others. In the context of reaching out to the lost and becoming a blessing to every tongue, tribe and nation, we are made acutely aware that money, power, fame and influence are limited. We need the goodness of God flowing through us; we need the fruit of the Spirit cultivated in us so that we can achieve the impossible. By doing so we will be alive and live life to the fullest.

The Importance of the Fruit of the Spirit

It is clear that an abundant life is not possible without the presence of God abiding with us and without the evidence of the fruit of the Spirit manifesting through us. It is impossible to live life abundantly if we are self-centered; we must have the love of God operating within us. It is only through His love that we can do the impossible. Without it we are forced to play it safe with blinders like domesticated horses, we can focus our eyes on our little patch of ground and spend the rest of our lives with this limited worldview. Then finally we die, not knowing that the whole world can be blessed through us.

The fruit of the Spirit is the only guarantee that we can have an abundant life. Take for instance the effect of not having joy. If we don't have it then we cannot function properly. We all, even without degrees in psychology or medicine, understand the negative impact of melancholy, and the debilitating affect it has on our mind and body.

The same is true if we don't have peace. If our hearts and minds are troubled then we cannot rest. If we cannot rest then we cannot sleep and are then deprived of our decision-making capabilities. We become irritable and in short we become unproductive. You may sleep in a bed worth tens of thousands of dollars, but if you don't have peace you might as well sleep on the floor. The softest cushion in the world will never give you the rest you desperately need.

Patience, kindness, gentleness, self-control and goodness are just byproducts of love, joy and peace made real in our lives. If we develop these things, then we have the capability to succeed and at the same time have the capacity to sustain it. We will never become like the rich fool who worked all his life but never enjoyed the fruits of his labor. More tragically is the fact that he was not able to share it with others. We are called to exhibit the goodness of God. If we know how to become channels of God's blessings then we have come to understand what it truly means to live life to the fullest. The goodness of God must not be hoarded it must be shared. This is only possible if we have the fruit of the Spirit.

An abundant life does not consist of power, wealth and fame. It is defined rather by our ability to live in accordance with the will of God. An abundant life is also defined by our obedient heart, willing to obey God's commands. It is seen in the depth of our service to others.

When we listen to the words of Jesus, we receive His eternal life and become citizens of His kingdom. As we continue to press on and passionately persevere to learn more of Christ, this is what is in store for us according to His word:

"I am the true vine, and My Father is the vinedresser. Every branch in Me that does not bear fruit He takes away; and every branch that bears fruit He prunes, that it may bear more fruit. You are already clean because of the word which I have spoken to you. Abide in Me, and I in you. As the branch cannot bear fruit of itself, unless it abides in the vine, neither can you, unless you abide in Me. I am the vine, you are the branches. He who abides in Me, and I in him, bears much fruit; for without Me you can do nothing. If anyone does not abide in Me, he is cast out as a branch and is withered; and they gather them and throw them into the fire, and they are burned. If you abide in Me, and My words abide in you, you will ask what you desire, and it shall be done for you. By this My Father is glorified, that you bear much fruit; so you will be My disciples. As the Father loved Me, I also have loved you; abide in My love" (John 15:1-9).

When we listen and obey, we become the disciples of Jesus Christ and His Spirit dwells in us. We become fruitful beyond imagination. The Apostle Paul talked about this, "But the fruit of the Spirit is love, joy, peace, longsuffering, kindness, goodness, faithfulness, gentleness, self-control. Against such there is no law" (Galatians 5:22,23). We can only have abundant life when we abide in Him, in His words and in His love! As we abide in Him, the Holy Spirit will reproduce the fruit of the Spirit in us, which is actually the character of Jesus Christ.

The Importance of the Fruit of Goodness

Love is at the heart of this fruit. Everything is made possible because of God's love. We experience abundant life because we no longer see the world in a mindset of lust, greed, hate and fear. God has chosen us to be His vessels of goodness so that the whole earth will be blessed through the works of His people. We need the goodness of God to be cultivated in us by the Holy Spirit so that we can achieve the impossible. By doing so, we will live life to the fullest.

Reflect and Discuss

Which fruit(s) do you need to grow in the most?

How will you work on that?

CHAPTER NINE

Receiving the Goodness of God and Delighting in it

2 Chronicles 6:41, "Now therefore, Arise, O Lord God, to Your resting place, You and the ark of Your strength. Let Your priests, O Lord God, be clothed with salvation, and let Your saints rejoice in goodness."

We are His saints therefore: we can receive God's goodness. He has good news. He has good contents. He has good promises. He has good works. Man, He is good! We don't have to achieve His goodness!! We receive it.

God Has Good News for Us to Receive

The gospel is good news. In a world full of bad news, God has good news. Jesus Christ is the good news. The good news of the gospel that Jesus brings is that mankind can be redeemed from sin by the life, death and resurrection of Jesus Christ. In Luke 2:10,11 an angel said, "...Do not be afraid, for behold, I bring you good tidings of great joy which will be to all people. For there is born to you this day in the city of David a Savior, who is Christ the Lord." Jesus came to save us from our sins and give us eternal life. John 1:11-13, "He came to His own, and His own did not receive Him. But as many as received Him, to them He gave the right to become children of God, to those who believe in His name: who were born, not of blood, nor of the will of the flesh, nor of the will of man, but of God." If we receive Jesus Christ as Lord and Savior, receive the message of His good news; He gives us the right or authority to become His child. We turn from our sin (repent) and turn to God to receive the gift that was purchased for us by His death on the cross. Now that is good news – that is great news! His goodness is for everyone.

God Has Good Gifts for Us

God is a good Father and gives good gifts to His children. God loves us so much. He's really "crazy" in love with us and He has given us the gift of salvation and also other gifts. James 1:17, "Every good gift and every perfect gift is from above, and comes down from the Father of lights, with whom there is no variation or shadow of turning." Part of fulfilling God's good pleasure is to operate in the gifts of the Spirit. Psalm 68:18, "You have ascended on high, you have led captivity captive; you have received gifts among men, even from the rebellious, that the Lord God might dwell there." In Ephesians 4, Paul quotes this verse and states in verse 8 that when Christ ascended on high, He led captivity captive and gave gifts to men. Paul goes on to explain in Ephesians 4:11-16 that the five-fold ministry gifts (apostles, prophets, evangelists, pastors and teachers) are "for the equipping of the saints for the work of ministry, for the edifying of the body of Christ, till we all come to the unity of the faith and of the knowledge of the Son of God, to a perfect man, to the measure of the stature of the fullness of Christ." It goes on to say that as each part in the body does its share, the body builds itself up in love. You have a share… you have a part in the body of Christ…you can use your gifts and bring God pleasure and the body gets built up (edified) in love! In Romans 12:1-8, the motivational gifts of the Spirit are serving, teaching, giving, exhortation, administration, mercy and prophecy. Each person is motivated by the gifts God has given them. In 1 Corinthians 12:1-11, the manifestational gifts of the Spirit are tongues, interpretation of tongues, prophecy, faith, healing, miracles, knowledge, wisdom and discerning spirits. If you study the gifts, you will begin to discover, develop and deploy the gifts God has given you. Receive the gifts of the Spirit. God has good gifts for you.

Every good gift comes from our good heavenly Father. He is pleased when we unlock His goodness by releasing and using the gifts of the Spirit. Each of us is gifted by God to share His love and ministry. 1 Corinthians 1:4-7 says, "I thank my God always concerning you for the grace of God which was given to you by Christ Jesus, that you were enriched in everything by Him in all utterance and all knowledge, even as the testimony of Christ was confirmed in you, so that you come short in no gift, eagerly waiting for the revelation of our Lord Jesus Christ." The Corinthians were enriched with gifts of the Spirit which confirmed Christ was in their midst. When we allow Christ to move in our midst, the Father is pleased. It is good…His goodness!

Over the years I have loved watching the gifts of the Spirit please the Father and bless His people. A word of knowledge can really encourage a person to know God is with them and directing them. A prophecy can build up, comfort and encourage another. When someone gets healed, when the gift of faith operates and people get to see miracles happen, it blesses God. As you know how God has gifted you, it will help you discern His will for your life. Each one's gifts are to be used for the benefit of others.

God Has Good Promises for You

God's goodness is seen in His good promises, which He has for you and for me. In Nehemiah 9:25, God says, "And they took strong cities and a rich land, and possessed houses full of all goods, cisterns already dug, vineyards, olive groves, and fruit trees in abundance. So they ate and were filled and grew fat, and delighted themselves in Your great goodness." God wants us to delight in His great goodness. How do we delight in His great goodness? By receiving His love, grace, promises and

His goodness. Stop right now and say, "Father, in the Name of Jesus, I receive Your love and goodness."

God made promises to David. 1 Chronicles 17:26 says, "And now, Lord, You are God, and have promised this goodness to Your servant." The Ark was brought back to Jerusalem and worship was organized. God's promise to David was accomplished. God wants to fulfill His promises to us as we meet the conditions of the promises. Delight yourself in His great goodness as He fulfills His promises to you!

All of the promises of God are yes and amen in Him (2 Chronicles 1:20)! Yes and Amen!! What promises are you waiting on today?

Reflect and Discuss

What can you delight and rejoice in regarding God's goodness?

Receive God's promise. What are some promises God has given you? Write them out and thank God for the answer!

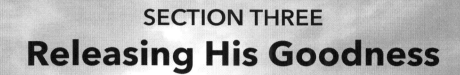

SECTION THREE
Releasing His Goodness

RELEASING THE GOODNESS OF GOD AS JESUS DID

RELEASING THE GOODNESS OVERCOMES EVIL

RELEASING THE GOODNESS OF GOD TO THE NATIONS

CHAPTER TEN

Releasing the Goodness of God as Jesus Did

Acts 10:38, "How God anointed Jesus of Nazareth with the Holy Spirit and with power, who went about doing good and healing all who were oppressed by the devil, for God was with Him."

I am moved by Dr. Luke's account in the Book of Acts. He tells the things that Jesus began to do and teach. His account is full of the great things that God continued to do through the apostles and disciples of the Lord Jesus Christ. Jesus was the one who released the goodness of God.

Jesus of Nazareth was anointed by God the Father with the Holy Spirit and with power. The key to the ministry of Jesus was His working together with the Holy Spirit. He did only what he saw the Father and the Holy Spirit doing in His life and ministry. John 5:19,20, "Then Jesus answered and said to them, 'Most assuredly, I say to you, the Son can do nothing of Himself, but what He sees the Father do; for whatever He does, the Son also does in like manner. For the Father loves the Son, and shows Him all things that He Himself does; and He will show Him greater works than these, that you may marvel." This demonstrates how Jesus worked with the Father and what He was doing. For John 5:30 says, "I can of Myself do nothing. As I hear, I judge; and My judgment is righteous, because I do not seek My own will but the will of the Father who sent Me." Jesus was totally dependent on the Spirit of God to speak to Him, Jesus' whole life was devoted to doing good and healing people who were oppressed of the devil!

In the midst of a rural town called Nazareth, stands an old synagogue. It is big enough to accommodate both young and old men – including the teenagers who had already completed their Bar Mitzvahs. They go there when it is time for worship and reading the Word of God. The outside walls are worn from the onslaught of the elements, but the interior is well kept and conducive to hold teaching and reading sessions. It is at its finest every Sabbath day, when men from all walks of life descend upon here and spend the whole morning exhorting each other to follow the commandments of God as communicated through Moses in Mount Sinai. This particular synagogue is special because it is witness to a peculiar occurrence, which is the steady transformation of a local Boy as He grew up and demonstrated that He has received favor before man and God. He is known locally as Jesus and for eighteen years now it is customary for Him to come to this place to hear the Rabbi talk about the Lord of heaven. But on this particular Sabbath day Jesus has come no longer as an ordinary resident of Nazareth, but as the Son of God. On this day, He entered the synagogue full of the Holy Spirit and on fire, ready to take on the world.

The sheer presence of the Lord and the authority that emanated from Him made the resident Rabbi gesture toward his assistant while at the same time pointing at the scroll sitting in the middle of the room. The dutiful servant lifted the scroll and then handed it to Jesus. It was the scroll of the prophet Isaiah that was given to Him. Jesus took it, began to read and unbeknown to many He is not only reading, He is also declaring something very important, and He said:

"The Spirit of the Lord is upon Me, because He has anointed Me to preach the gospel to the poor; He has sent Me to heal the brokenhearted, to proclaim liberty to the captives and recovery of sight to the blind, to set at liberty those who are oppressed; to proclaim the acceptable year of the Lord" (Luke 4:18,19).

After reading, Jesus handed to scroll back to the attendant. The eyes of everyone in the building were intently focused on Him because they were eager to hear how Jesus would explain God's Word to them. For many decades these old Nazarenes had been discussing the meaning and significance of this passage taken from the book of Isaiah. They knew that it spoke about the coming Messiah. They were also familiar with the signs of His coming: the Spirit of the Lord would be upon Him and He would perform wondrous works, as well as heal blind eyes and set captives free.

Those who were in attendance wanted Jesus to encourage them, to spur them on to be patient in waiting for the arrival of the Messiah. But Jesus did not expound on the text and He did not inspire them to set their eyes on a future hope, a soon-to-come Savior and Lord. Instead, He met their gaze and made this proclamation: "…Today this scripture is fulfilled in your hearing" (Luke 4:21). The Bible says that the people were amazed; a new day dawned.

This passage is a flashback of the first few days of Jesus' ministry. He later left Nazareth to demonstrate that He was indeed the much awaited Lord and Savior of Israel. But more importantly, He moved quickly from town to town because He had a schedule to keep, for at the end of a three year period He would offer Himself as a sacrifice to destroy the power of sin. In the midst of His ministry, an interesting development occurred. He was not even halfway into it when He began to train disciples, to take over when His time was up, when He had to go back to His Father in heaven.

Jesus was not interested in building a congregation of hearers only but also a group of workers willing to collaborate with Him so that His Father's Kingdom may be established on earth and His will be done in the lives of every man, woman and child. In the 21st century nothing has changed, it is the same goal, quest and the same Lord. Nevertheless, the question for this generation is this: Are we in agreement with the Lord?

Not to Be Served and Not to Lord it Over Them

We thought that making disciples was easy for Peter, James, John and the rest of Jesus' crew. We have taken it for granted, assuming that it was always this way. But the truth is the followers of Christ had their own selfish agenda. They were expecting a king to rule over them and to establish a monarchical system of governance in Palestine. After all, Jesus said that the Kingdom of God is near. Against this backdrop, the twelve primary followers of Christ were in anticipation of a government structure wherein Jesus was the absolute ruler and they were the privileged enforcers of His laws. Never in their wildest dreams did they look forward to a lifetime of service and to walk this earth as Jesus did.

They were in for the surprise of their life when Jesus died, rose from the grave and left them here on this planet. The only consolation they received was the evidence of an invisible Kingdom: however, all the members of that Kingdom are not seen as princesses and Lords but servants. They were followers whose lives were patterned after their Master, who once said that the greatest among them is the servant of all. Although they were childish at first Jesus taught them well, He lead by example and at the end He gave His life to make a forceful and positive statement that love is the only key. At the end the apostles realized that they must stay here on earth, not to be served and not to Lord it over other people but to release the goodness of God just as Jesus did.

You Will Do Greater Things than These

As we go deeper into this revelation it is easy to be astounded by the magnitude of God's work and at the same time we have to wonder why He has entrusted us with so much. When we talk about releasing God's goodness on the earth we are not merely paying lip service. We are not simply aspiring to perform obligatory, charitable works to our fellowmen, such as giving money to the poor, helping the orphans and even performing socially responsible tasks. When we dare to become channels of the Lord's blessings we actually desire to be like Him. And this is how the Bible described some of Jesus' signature moves:

"And Jesus went about all Galilee, teaching in their synagogues, preaching the gospel of the kingdom, and healing all kinds of sickness and all kinds of disease among the people. Then His fame went throughout all of Syria; and they brought to Him all sick people who were afflicted with various diseases and torments, and those who were demon-possessed, epileptics, and paralytics; and He healed them. Great multitudes followed him – from Galilee, and from Decapolis, Jerusalem, Judea, and beyond the Jordan" (Matthew 4:23-25).

There are many passages that talk about the same thing (see Mark 3:8-10 and Luke 4:40,41). However, Matthew's recollection of how Jesus released God's goodness is more detailed and layered than the others and therefore deserves more scrutiny. Consider how Matthew summarized Jesus' ministry using the following terms:

Teaching and Preaching

Good News of the Kingdom

Healing every disease and sickness

Healing those suffering from severe pain

Healing the paralyzed

Casting out demons

Large crowds followed him

Even if we simply focused on one aspect of the said passage and only took a bird's eye view of Matthew's gospel, we cannot help but be astonished at the depth and breadth of Jesus' ministry and how He remedied the problems of this world as He became the embodiment of God's goodness on the earth. He worked hard to bless the people and acted far beyond what was expected of the Messiah. The Israelites simply anticipated a liberator and perhaps a king in the image of David, but they never thought that He would come like Jesus came.

For the 21st century Church we need to be reminded that Jesus did not simply preach and teach. It seems that a majority of Christian denominations mastered the ability to teach and preach about how to become a good follower of Jesus and how to become good citizens in their respective countries. We are masters when it comes to the moral issues of the land. We are not saying that we have attained perfection, but we have devoted a significant amount of time and resources to teaching and preaching about the law. We have forgotten that there is more to Christianity than merely attending church meetings once a week.

We have to mature in our faith as we try to emulate our Lord, for He made it very clear to us that we ought to do the same. Jesus said, "Most assuredly, I say to you, he who believes in Me, the works that I do he will do also; and greater works than these he will do, because I go to My Father" (John 14:12). It is, therefore, necessary to go over what Matthew said and find out if we are doing what Jesus expected us to do. Let us look at it as if it is a sticky note that Jesus posted on our refrigerator door, reminding us that we can still improve our game.

The first question to ask ourselves is this: Am I preaching the message of the Kingdom? When we say we are preaching the "good news of the Kingdom," we are not merely discussing the benefits that we can get from Christianity but also how we can demonstrate the reality of the Lord's Prayer that states: "Let Your Kingdom come, let Your Will be done on earth as it is in heaven." In other words, can we produce tangible proof that somewhere beyond our Universe is the Kingdom of our Lord? Jesus was able to do that and so should we.

The second question that we have to ask ourselves is: Am I willing to become a channel of blessings when it pertains to healing every manner of sickness and disease among the people in our community? This requires boldness and faith as well as the knowledge that we have this capability through the grace of our Lord Jesus Christ. Imagine the magnitude of

God's goodness that will be released if we allow God to use us in this ministry and not just be limited to the preaching and the teaching of the Word. Besides, if we are serious to learn more about the pure gospel of Christ, we have to venture into the realm of supernatural healing.

The third question that we have to ask ourselves is: Why is it that Matthew differentiated the healing of sickness and disease to the healing of severe pain; the healing of paralysis; and the healing of demon possession? One possible answer is that these three types of maladies have different root causes. The first root is due to harmful microorganisms, the second is the result of injury, the third is caused by a malfunctioning organ and the last is caused by a demonic attack. We can therefore argue that the clarification through a detailed analysis of the problems of humanity show God's desire to answer specific prayers and target specific problems. We should do the same. Think of how the Lord's name will be glorified throughout the earth if we are willing to walk this path.

The fourth question that we have to ask ourselves is: Am I willing to step out of my comfort zone and embrace the crowds? Before you say yes, please frame your answer with the knowledge of what Jesus had to deal with when He immersed Himself in a sea of humanity desperate for His healing touch and spiritual guidance. This is what the Bible has to say regarding what we can expect out there: "Then the multitude came together again, so that they could not so much as eat bread" (Mark 3:20).

The number of people was so numerous they were pressing in on Jesus. We remember a similar incident wherein Jesus instructed His followers to prepare the boat because the people kept pressing on Him until He was finally pushed to the sea and so He climbed aboard to commence preaching. So how crowded can it be? The Bible tells us that in one healing crusade a mob surrounded a house in such a way that no one could enter through the door and windows. Thus, the friends of a paralyzed man had to destroy part of the roof to lower him down to where Jesus stood.

The last statement in Mark 3:20 speaks volumes of the personal sacrifice that Jesus had to undergo in order to release God's goodness to the multitudes. He and His disciples were working from dawn to dusk and with such intensity that they even forgot to take a lunch break. The commotion as well as the passion displayed every time Jesus embraced the crowds was so intense that Jesus' biological family could not help but express their concern and they wanted to take charge of Him. In every day terms they wanted to kidnap Jesus, bring Him home and place Him in seclusion in order to protect Him from the very people He was trying to help. It is almost impossible to accept the idea that we who are mere mortals are given the same call. We are commanded to release the goodness of God not only to our friends and people from our local church, but to outsiders who are longing for the same supernatural touch from God.

Releasing the Goodness of God Like Jesus Christ

We are left reeling from the impact of Jesus' directives regarding the need for us to emulate His desires, actions and methods. While we are still figuring out if we have what it takes to become vessels that can carry and contain the glory of God, Jesus dropped another atomic-bomb-revelation in our laps. He did not say that we can merely aspire to be holy copycats, He also made a promise that His followers can expect more, for He said, "….and greater works than these he will do, because I go to My Father" (John 14:12). This additional information is well beyond our strength and abilities. We have to wonder if it is even remotely possible to surpass the ministry of Jesus.

We need to consult the Bible once again to find out if this thing can be accomplished. As we review the ministry of Jesus Christ we will notice that the gospel writers and even the Apostle Paul are of one mind when it comes to the explanation of Jesus' power source. A typical explanation reads: "That word you know, which was proclaimed throughout all Judea, and began from Galilee after the baptism which John preached: how God anointed Jesus of Nazareth with the Holy Spirit and with power, who went about doing good and healing all who were oppressed by the devil, for God was with Him" (Acts 10:37,38).

We are encouraged by Luke's commentary. Jesus was able to do all those things because He was baptized, anointed with the Holy Spirit and power and God was with Him. After reading this, we still need faith and boldness to enter into the supernatural realm but somehow we know what to do. The Apostle Paul provided another reason why we can equal and even surpass the ministry of Christ:

"But if the ministry of death, written and engraved on stones, was glorious, so that the children of Israel could not look steadily at the face of Moses because of the glory of his countenance, which glory was passing away, how will the ministry of the Spirit not be more glorious? For if the ministry of condemnation had glory, the ministry of righteousness exceeds much more in glory. For even what was made glorious had no glory in this respect, because of the glory that excels. For if what is passing away was glorious, what remains is much more glorious" (2 Corinthians 3:7-11).

There are at least three things to glean from this passage. First, we are brought from glory to glory as our Lord continues to reveal Himself to us from one generation to the next. Second, we don't need to begin from scratch because God was so gracious to make a covenant with the Israelites and through them He was able to show Himself to the world. It was the Israelites who first took hold of the Commandments and through the spectacular works of His hands like the pillar of cloud by day and the pillar of fire by night, as well as a supernatural creation of a mighty nation who citizens were former slaves in Egypt. And finally, there is a much better covenant available for us today that makes possible a phenomenon described by St. Paul as: The Ministry of the Spirit. And according to the good apostle this ministry is even more glorious, because aside from the capacity to create signs and wonders, it is also a ministry that can help people attain righteousness. This explains Jesus' profound statement when He said that we can do greater things after He is gone back to His Father in heaven. This is because this action signifies that He has died on the cross, resurrected from the grave and paid for our sins.

This is a concrete basis as to the need to emulate the ministry of Jesus Christ. We know that we can and should follow His footsteps and even more importantly to surpass what He has done during His three-year ministry on this earth. But instead of struggling to understand how we can accomplish a seemingly impossible task, we are now comforted and assured by the knowledge that we are not doing the work but the Holy Spirit. In fact we must rename our ministry and instead of calling it a ministry of Mr. So-and-So we now have to call it the ministry of the Spirit. In this regard we can say again the declaration made by our Lord in the beginning of His earthly work. Now, repeat after me: "The Spirit of the Lord God is on me, because He has anointed me to preach good news to the poor. He sent me to proclaim freedom for the prisoners and recovery of sight for the blind, to release the oppressed, to proclaim the year of the Lord's favor."

Continue to replay this utterance in your mind until you can see yourself speaking the very same words that Jesus did. This is possible because the Spirit of the Lord is upon us and it is He who has sent us. It is the Spirit and not human flesh that has commanded us to proclaim and then to release the goodness that we have seen from the Lord. We can release the goodness of God just as Jesus did when He was here on earth. We can do it because when the Spirit of the Lord is with us, it is the same as having Jesus by our side and we become mere spectators as we watch Him work in the midst of broken, sick and lost humanity.

God has anointed us with the Holy Spirit and power. We are anointed with the Holy Spirit and power to go about doing good. "The words 'doing good' are from the word euergeteo, which is an old word that denoted a benefactor, a philanthropist, or one who financially supported charitable work. This word would only be used to describe a person who possessed great financial substance and who used it to assist those who were less fortunate."[10] Jesus went about sharing the Father's resources with those who are in need. He not only supernaturally healed people, but was concerned with their natural needs. You and I can release God's goodness and work with Him to meet people's natural needs.

God has a heart to heal all those who have been oppressed by the devil. 1 John 3:8 says, "He who sins is of the devil, for the devil has sinned from the beginning. For this purpose the Son of God was manifested, that He might destroy the works of the devil." Jesus came to minister healing to those who need healing. All through the Gospels we can see the tremendous ministry of Jesus to release God's goodness through healing to broken and oppressed people. Matthew 9:35-38, "Then Jesus went about all the cities and villages, teaching in their synagogues, preaching the gospel of the kingdom, and healing every sickness and every disease among the people. But when He saw the multitudes, He was moved with compassion for them, because they were weary and scattered, like sheep having no shepherd. Then He said to His disciples, 'The harvest truly is plentiful, but the laborers are few. Therefore pray the Lord of the harvest to send out laborers into his harvest.'"

One such time God illuminated this passage to me, was while I was in Tanzania, having gone with Leif Hetland from Global Mission Awareness and an outreach team. We had gone out in the afternoon to hand out flyers for the crusade we were helping with in Dar es Salaam that was to begin that night. I had a bad attitude wondering why I had to be traipsing through the mud and filth to try and talk to people who spoke a different language than I. The Lord spoke to my heart and said, "You are doing this because I did this as I walked through cities and villages." I had to repent and ask God to forgive my attitude. Then I saw a beautiful sidewalk right in the middle of the mud and filth and my thought was, "What is this doing here?" The Lord spoke to me and said, "This is like My goodness." It led me to a beauty shop. A Muslim woman and her friend came out of the shop

---

10 Renver, Rick, *Sparkling Gems from the Greek*, Teach All Nations, Tulsa, OK © 2003, pg. 536.

and asked us to pray for her deaf daughter. When a group of us begin to pray in Jesus' name, she was healed! They came to the crusade and gave their lives to Jesus. We went home with a heart attitude to go to the villages and cities to release His goodness!

Reflect and Discuss

How can you release His goodness?

How does the enemy try and stop you from doing this?

CHAPTER ELEVEN

Releasing the Goodness of God Overcomes Evil

I love the book, 7 Men by Eric Metaxas. It is about seven great men and the secrets to their greatness. One of the seven was William Wilberforce, who lived from 1759 to 1833. Wilberforce changed the course of history and helped to abolish slavery. I heard my friend, Graham Cooke say once that Wilberforce had said, "Let's make goodness fashionable." Eric Metaxas in this book said, "The battle against the slave trade was largely won when a bill passed both houses of Parliament in 1897." Wilberforce knew that in order to get the votes he needed to win that particular battle, God would have to change the hearts and minds of people first and that was very much a cultural battle. This realization prompted Wilberforce to say that part of his strategy in fighting many of these social evils was to "make goodness fashionable." (Metaxas p. 50) We too overcome evil with good – God's goodness.

Practical Goodness

How can we "make goodness fashionable?" Jesus was quite fashionable. In Romans 12 the Apostle Paul talked about using our spiritual gifts and about showing practical love as Christians.

Romans 12:19-21, "Beloved, do not avenge yourselves, but rather give place to wrath; for it is written, 'Vengeance is Mine, I will repay,' says the Lord. Therefore 'If your enemy hungers, feed him; if he is thirsty, give him a drink; for in so doing you will heap coals of fire on his head.' Do not be overcome by evil, but overcome evil with good." Some may think that this passage has to do with burning the face of your enemy with hot coals. What Christ was saying here actually is about providing heat to cook with and to warm your enemy. During a time when you are being mistreated, this verse is saying to go out of your way to provide for the needs of your enemy.

One way to overcome evil with good is by feeding our enemy when he is hungry. Jesus, and Matthew 5:43-48, says, "You have heard that it was said, 'You shall love your neighbor and hate your enemy.' But I say to you, love your enemies, bless those who curse you, do good to those who hate you, and pray for those who spitefully use you and persecute you, that you may be sons of your Father in heaven; for He makes His sun rise on the evil and on the good, and sends rain on the just and on the unjust. For if you love those who love you, what reward have you? Do not even the tax collectors do the same? And if you greet your brethren only, what do you do more than others? Do not even the tax collectors do so? Therefore you shall be perfect, just as your Father in heaven is perfect." God's goodness and love is great! Loving our enemies by feeding them when they are hungry is one way we can touch their hearts and overcome evil with good.

Another way to overcome evil with good is to bless those who curse us. The story was told of Robert E. Lee, "Hearing General Lee speak in the highest terms to President Davis about a certain officer, another officer, greatly astonished, said to him, 'General, do you know that the man of whom you speak so highly to the President is one of your bitterest enemies, and misses no opportunity to malign you?' 'Yes,' replied General Lee, 'but the President asked my opinion of him; he did not ask for his opinion of me."[11] General Lee gave good for evil. This ties into what Jesus said in Matthew, quoted above, about blessing those who curse you. I have found it is wonderful to bless people even if they curse me and do not like me. When we are obedient and bless those who curse us, we resemble Abba Father!

In the Message by Eugene Peterson, it says this in Romans 12:19-21, "Don't insist on getting even; that's not for you to do. 'I'll do the judging,' says God. 'I'll take care of it.' Our Scriptures tell us that if you see our enemy hungry, go buy that person lunch, or if he's thirsty, get him a drink. Your generosity will surprise him with goodness. Don't let evil get the best of you; get the best of evil by doing good." In the New King James Version, it says in verse 20, "Therefore if your enemy is hungry, feed him; if he is thirsty, give him a drink; for in doing so, you will heap coals of fire on his head." What does that mean? Your showing and releasing goodness will affect them greatly.

Pearls from Peter and John

In the books of first and second Peter, there are great concepts of releasing God's goodness. The first pearl is found in 1 Peter 3:15-17, "But sanctify the Lord God in your hearts, and always be ready to give a defense to everyone who asks you a reason for the hope that is in you, with meekness and fear; having a good conscience, that when they defame you as evildoers, those who revile your good conduct in Christ may be ashamed. For it is better, if it is the will of God, to suffer for doing good than for doing evil." Peter says to be ready to be a witness and live the Christian life. It is better to suffer doing good in the will of God than doing evil.

The second pearl is found in 2 Peter 1:5, "But also for this very reason, giving all diligence, add to your faith virtue, to virtue knowledge." In the Spirit-filled Bible references "virtue, arete" are used in classical Greek "to describe any quality that elicited preeminent estimation for a person. Later the word signified

---

11 Encyclopedia of 7700 Illustrations #951 by Paul Lee Tan. Bible Communications Inc. © 1996 Electronic Edition.

intrinsic value, moral excellency, and goodness. It is used both of God (1 Peter 2:9) and persons (Philippians 4:8 and 2 Peter 1:3,5)."[12] You can release God's goodness everywhere you go.

The third pearl is found in 3 John 1:11,12, "Beloved, do not imitate what is evil, but what is good. He who does good is of God, but he who does evil has not seen God. Demetrius has a good testimony from all, and from the truth itself. And we also bear witness, and you know that our testimony is true." In this passage, John, the Apostle, says to imitate or follow the positive examples of godly people. He uses Demetrius as a good/positive example and Diotrephes as a bad example. We are all examples. We are either a good example or a bad example. As we follow the good example of Jesus, John and believers, we do good and release God's goodness.

The fourth pearl is found in 1 John 3:10,11, "In this the children of God and the children of the devil are manifest: Whoever does not practice righteousness is not of God, nor is he who does not love his brother. For this is the message that you heard from the beginning, that we should love one another." As we practice righteousness and loving our brothers and sisters in Christ we release the goodness of God. To practice righteousness is to do what is right.

May we realize that we overcome evil by doing good. Think of ways you can bring God's goodness into the darkness. Find someone who is hungry, help someone in need…There are so many ways to release God's goodness!

Reflect and Discuss

Who can you release God's goodness to today?

How can you release God's goodness into some evil situations?

---

12 The New Spirit-filled Bible, Jack Hayford, Executive Editor, Thomas Nelson Bibles, © 2002, Nashville, TN, pg. 1775.

CHAPTER TWELVE

Releasing the Goodness of God to the Nations

In 2013 alone, twenty-four million people will die from hunger and poverty and of that number 55,000 will die without hearing the name of Jesus at least once. This is because there are still 1600 people groups that are unreached, and 1.9 billion people are still ignorant of the fact that we carry the good news of the Kingdom, the gospel of Jesus Christ. It is time to release the goodness of God to the nations of the world. It is especially needed by the marginalized, poor, starving, uneducated, sick and lost, living in the darkest region of the world – in North Africa, the Middle East and Asia, an area known as the 10/40 window. If Jesus decided to come down once again, just as he did in Israel, you would find him ministering in this particular geographic zone. However, Jesus had a far better plan. He ascended to heaven to be reunited with His Father and then He released the Holy Spirit to be upon us so that He can exponentially increase the scope of His ministry. By working through us He can be in different nations at once; He is therefore counting on us to continue His work in this planet, until the earth is filled with the knowledge of the glory of the Lord just as the waters cover the sea (Habakkuk 2:14).

The fact that there are still more than 1,000 unreached people groups and hundreds of millions of others who are not yet able to call on the name of the Lord is proof that the god of this world has blinded many. It can also be said that many Christians are blinded in the sense that they cannot see the need and do not feel the burden to become part of the global mission movement which was started by Jesus two thousand years ago. The explanation for this lack of desire to become instruments of God's favor and blessing to a lost and dying humanity is rooted in the major misunderstanding of the Word of God.

The Need of the Nations

We usually read the Bible with the mindset of a consumer, eager to discover something of value and then utilize it to bring wealth, comfort, enjoyment and peace of mind. As mentioned in previous chapters there's nothing seriously wrong with this attitude except that the Bible is not a primary manual to overcome poverty, a book full of tips on how to succeed in the marketplace, or literature filled with wise sayings. The Bible was written to reveal God's plan of redemption and to reveal His goodness.

In this universe there is no longer any argument over who is ruler and king. There is no battle that has yet to be fought to settle once and for all who owns the cosmos. This issue has been resolved since the very beginning. Therefore, if we are slow to acknowledge His Lordship then there is no connection with him. We are not under His dominion. In short we live outside His Kingdom. We have to enter into His heavenly realm through a re-birth in the Spirit.

Why then did David choose the shepherd-sheep relationship? He could have said that Yahweh is Lord and we must be under His authority. But David explicitly said that the Lord is his Shepherd. There is something more to this relationship than meets the eye.

A shepherd, as a king, owns property. A shepherd can be a possessor of a variety of things. He may own a house, some tools, clothes, cooking utensils, an orchard and much more. These things are important to him but among his various possessions there is nothing that can rival the value that he places on his sheep. The flock is his special possession, the one thing that gives him much joy. If only his farm implements could transform themselves into sheep, they would do so in a heartbeat. If only his cow could transform itself into a sheep, it would not hesitate for a moment.

When the Lord gave the reason why He wanted the Hebrew slaves freed, He said, "'Now therefore, if you will indeed obey My voice and keep My covenant, then you shall be a special treasure to Me above all people; for all the earth is Mine. And you shall be to Me a kingdom of priests and a holy nation.' These are the words which you shall speak to the children of Israel" (Exodus 19:5,6). There are two key statements here in relation to our discussion. God said, "The whole earth is Mine." He also said, "You will be My treasured possession." Thus, God is not forced to exert His authority. Whether we like it or not we are already under His dominion. But because of His infinite wisdom, He provided a way for us to have the free will to choose. It is only by choosing Him we can be locked into His embrace and be elevated above the other creatures under His rulership. This is exactly why the Hebrew slaves had to cross the desert before entering the Promised Land. The wilderness purified their hearts, as they were about to make the most important decision of their lives: whether to follow God or to go back and be slaves. In order to enjoy the benefits that come from the Shepherd-sheep relationship, one must first submit to the Lordship of the Shepherd.

In Scripture, the books known as "the law" express the commandments of God and what He needed to accomplish and establish here on earth. "The Prophets" is the term used to describe the body of writing attributed to the prophets of Isreal. But a prophet is merely a spokesperson of God and he cannot say anything except the desires and intentions of the Lord. Prophets merely echo the commands of God. Therefore, when we read the Bible using this new understanding, then we will begin to correctly divide the word of truth to reveal the desires and intentions of God and not just read it as another self-help book.

Let us ask the Jews how they view the Word of God. Their answer will provide the correct perspective. This is what they label the collection of scrolls from Genesis to Malachi: The Law and the Prophets (Matthew 22:40). In other words, the Bible is the expressed desires of God in written form.

The Abrahamic Covenant

The stories in the Bible were written in such a way that the dialogue and interaction of the people help reveal God's will on earth. Let us take a look at the life of Abraham. He is known as the "Father of Many Nations" in Genesis 17:1-7 we read, "When Abram was ninety-nine years old, the Lord appeared to Abram and said to him, 'I am Almighty God; walk before Me and be blameless. And I will make My covenant between Me and you, and will multiply you exceedingly." Then Abram fell on his face, and God talked with him, saying, 'As for Me, behold, My covenant is with you, and you shall be a father of many nations. No longer shall your name be called Abram, but your name shall be Abraham; for I have made you a father of many nations. I will make you exceedingly fruitful; and I will make nations of you, and kings shall come from you. And I will establish My covenant between Me and you and your descendants after you and their generations, for an everlasting covenant, to be God to you and your descendants after you."

Earlier, in Genesis 12:1-3, God has given instructions to Abraham, "Now the Lord had said to Abram: "Get out of your country from your family and from your father's house, to a land that I will show you. I will make you a great nation; I will bless you and make your name great; and you shall be a blessing. I will bless those who bless you, and I will curse him who curses you; and in you all the families of the earth shall be blessed."

He wants all the families of the earth to be blessed by Abraham's descendants. We inherited the same promise according to Paul's word in Galatians 3:14, "That the blessing of Abraham might come up on the Gentiles in Christ Jesus, that we might receive the promise of the Spirit through faith." It is to be carried on through us as Abraham's seed. Galatians 3:29 says, "And if you are Christ's, then you are Abraham's seed, and heirs according to the promise."

God has been building through the centuries from Abraham to see sons and daughters born into His Kingdom. As Abraham was, we are called to bless all the families of the earth. That is why the Lord Jesus said in Matthew 28:18-20, "...All authority has been given to Me in heaven and on earth. Go therefore and make disciples of all the nations, baptizing them in the name of the Father and of the Son and of the Holy Spirit, teaching them to observe all things that I have commanded you; and lo, I am with you always, even to the end of the age.' Amen." Just think, it all began with one man's obedience – Abraham. Oh, yes, he made mistakes, but God honored his faith. We are channels of the goodness...the good news of the gospel of Jesus Christ.

The Psalmist David proclaims His goodness to the nations. Saul was hunting David down and it appears to be one of David's dark moments in life. David was hiding in a cave. He composed a song, this psalm, Psalm 57. In verse 2 he asked for help and in verse 4 he described his predicament; however, look what he wrote in Psalm 57:5: "Be exalted, O God, above the heavens; let Your glory be above all the earth." And then, look in Psalm 57:9, where he writes, "I will praise You, O Lord, among the peoples; I will sing to you among the nations."

What is least known is that Abraham was chosen by God to act as a channel of blessings to all the peoples of the earth. It was not a casual command, because the moment Yahweh released this specific command very early in the Bible, it changed the tone of the whole book. The way the Bible was written later began to change radically and everything that was recorded in it, from the beginning to the Book of Revelation, can be linked to what God said to Abraham that day, and this is the Lord's expressed desire in written form, "...Get out of your country, from your family and from your father's house, to a land that I will show you. I will make you a great nation; I will bless you and make your name great; and you shall be a blessing. I will bless those who bless you, and I will curse those who curse you; and in you all the families of the earth shall be blessed" (Genesis 12:1-3).

Our parents taught us not to interrupt someone while they are still talking. Sometimes that is easy to do, but sometimes you can't wait to butt in. In our excitement and the need to react to what was spoken, we sometimes appear rude. Let's say God is speaking to you right this very moment, do you have the temerity to butt in while the Almighty is still speaking? You will never do such a thing. But how many times have you read the above-mentioned passage without taking everything in completely, without hearing Him out until the end?

We easily taken verses one, two and three quarters of verse three, then we stop. Yes it is true, we read through it but we only meditate on the parts that are beneficial to us. Like an excited listener, we cut off the Lord, not by interrupting Him in the middle of His speech but by turning around, rejoicing, jumping up-and-down in the air because we had laid claim to the promises made to Abraham and made it our own. Yes, we have the right to inherit these promises because we too are children of Abraham by faith (Galatians 3:7). Nevertheless, we can only obtain these promises of blessing, honor and greatness if we are willing to take in everything, especially the last statement.

In the Abrahamic Covenant God provides an explanation as to why. This is a typical speech coming from the Lord of Hosts. He often gives a command with a promise. Yet, in this case God not only gives a command and promise, He also provided an explanation why He gave the command and promise in the first place. Thus, the covenant He made with Abraham was never intended to solely bless one individual or one family but all the families of the world. In fact, we must read God's declaration to Abraham with this in mind and then we understand the Lord's intentions. He was like a builder constructing something layer by layer. In other words, His first sentence leads to others. For example, the command to leave Abraham's homeland leads to inheriting a new country; the command to inhabit the land of promise will result in tremendous blessing; the blessings received will make Abraham great and at the same time increase his level of influence. But keep in mind that all of these lead to one thing: Abraham and his descendants will have the opportunity and capability to bless the peoples of the earth (Genesis 12:3).

This is one of the most important events in human history and it was made possible by God's command to go, and then by the obedience of one man to leave a place of comfort and security to travel to a foreign land, cross boundaries and then step into another culture. Therefore, we can never reap the fullness of God's rewards if we simply hoard what little blessing and influence we have right now and refuse to share it with others. We are blessed for one simple reason: to become channels of blessing and not merely to build storehouses to hoard our gain. This is perhaps the explanation of the Parable of the Rich Fool and why Jesus interjected that we must watch out for all kinds of greed. Therefore, greed kills, but generosity breeds life. It is time to open our hearts and minds to become radically generous and release God's blessings to the nations.

The Christian Missionary Enterprise: From Abraham to St. Paul

We tend to overlook the last portion of the Abrahamic covenant, but it is something for which we are not entirely to blame. Even the direct descendants of Abraham failed to honor this portion of the agreement. Abraham's firstborn was Isaac and from Isaac came Jacob who was the father of the twelve tribes of Israel. The whole clan took refuge in Egypt in the time of a severe famine but they ended up as slaves. Moses came in 400 years later to become God's chief instrument of deliverance and through his effort and that of his assistant Joshua, the Israelites were able to go back to Canaan, the land of Abraham, Isaac and Jacob.

It was perhaps the need to survive in a hostile land surrounded by their enemies that the Israelites were forced to become self-centered and mindful only of their own business. Even after Joshua succeeded in creating a home for them by carving a territory within Canaan large enough to sustain the twelve tribes of Israel, there was no evidence that they remembered the covenant made between God and their father Abraham. They even turned their back on God and completely forgot that they were the chosen people who will change the world.

As we read through the Book of Judges we can almost hear the deafening silence as the Israelites continue to demonstrate their ignorance of these things. It took a "man after God's own heart" to rediscover that Yahweh longs for the whole earth and not just Israel. David was so in tune with God's heart that he was able to decipher the secrets of the Lord. In his life and writings, David was able to express what he believed to be God's innermost desires and because he wanted to be constantly in pursuit of the Almighty, he did not hesitate to echo what he heard when he was in the presence of God. One day, he faced a giant of a man who defied the armies of Israel. David stood in the gap between the chosen people and their enemies who wanted to terrorize and enslave them. What he declared before he defeated Goliath revealed how intertwined his heart was with that of his Lord and King. For this is what David said, "This day the Lord will deliver you into my hand, and I will strike you and take your head from you. And this day I will give the carcasses of the camp of the Philistines to the birds of the air and the wild beasts of the earth, that all the earth may know that there is a God in Israel" (1 Samuel 17:46).

Unless you are familiar with the Abrahamic covenant, there is no way that you can understand what David said. If we were in David's shoes we would not choose as a war cry the declaration that the whole world will know that there is a God in Israel. Before you make the suggestion that perhaps the reason for David's speech is due to his deep piety, consider another bizarre announcement that seemingly has no connection with his present situation. When Saul was hunting him down like a common criminal and David went through one of the darkest moments of his life, David hid in the cave (see Psalm 57). In deep sorrow he composed a song and you kind of expect him to ask for help (Psalm 57:2) and also to describe his predicament (Psalm 57:4); however, you will never expect him to insert these statements into the song that he wrote, "Be exalted, O God, above the heavens; let Your glory be over all the earth" (Psalm 57:5). "I will praise you, O Lord, among the peoples; I will sing to You among the nations" (Psalm 57:9).

These verses and lines seem out of place. Don't you agree? When we are in a desperate situation we automatically feel we earn the license to be selfish. It is an instinct called self-preservation that takes over our being. In this particular Psalm we can see that David gave a portion of his thoughts and energy to pray for the whole earth. To share what he knew about his Creator and reveal it to the nations, specifically to foreigners. Simply put, David refused to be drawn into self-pity and instead he dug deep within himself to muster the strength to pray not only for himself but also for the nations. Obviously, David had access to information regarding how to draw the attention of God and how to open the windows of heaven so that he would be able to receive help, mercy and kindness from the Lord.

Until the Earth is Filled with the Knowledge of the Glory of the Lord

Let us place side-by-side Scriptures from the Abrahamic covenant, David's declaration when he fought Goliath and Psalm 57. We discover the common denominator between all three. To our great surprise the assurance of blessing, victory and salvation can be had if we demonstrate our willingness to declare the glory of the Lord to the nations of the earth.

If you were still in doubt remember how God blessed Abraham so that he became the father of many nations and how he became so great that kings learned from him about the wonderful God he served. This same principle can also be seen in the life of Solomon who became rich and powerful so that he could attract foreign rulers and dignitaries to come into his kingdom sharing with them his revelations about the one true God.

So, what then is a central message of the Old Testament, or as previously stated the Law and the Prophets? We know the answer to this question because an expert of the law asked Jesus, saying, "Teacher, which is the great commandment in the law?" (Matthew 22:36). Jesus replied, "...You shall love the Lord your God with all your heart, with all your soul, and with all your mind. This is the first and great commandment. And the second is like it: 'You shall love your neighbor as yourself. On these two commandments hang all the Law and the Prophets'" (Matthew 22:37-40).

Jesus clarified, once and for all, that the Word of God must not be utilized solely for selfish reasons. It is impossible to look at how Jesus simplified the entire Old Testament and not see the directive to focus our eyes unto the Lord and then afterwards to turn our attention to others. Before we move on, let us be reminded that this is a command from God. However, this is not a command without a promise. The blessing promised to Abraham and the victory and salvation experienced by David are made available to us as long as we continue to honor our part of the covenant, which is to become channels of God's blessing to the nations of the earth. Before Jesus ascended back to heaven He spoke of a similar thing: "All authority has been given to Me in heaven and on earth. Go therefore and make disciples of all the nations, baptizing them in the name of the Father and of the Son and of the Holy Spirit, teaching them to observe all things that I have commanded you; and lo, I am with you always, even to the end of the age. Amen" (Matthew 28:18-24).

Paul, the apostle, was a great man in history; he is one of my heroes. He came from a Jewish background, but was called to be an apostle to the Gentiles. His great desire was to proclaim the gospel of the Kingdom to the nations: Israel and the Gentile nations. In Romans 1:14-16 Paul states, "I am a debtor both to Greeks and to barbarians, both to wise and to unwise. So, as much as it is in me, I am ready to preach the gospel to you who are in Rome also. For I am not ashamed of the gospel of Christ, for it is the power of God to salvation for everyone who believes, for the Jew first and also for the Greek." Paul's heart was for everyone to know Jesus Christ as Lord and Savior through the message of the gospel of the Kingdom.

The goodness of God is released through the gospel of the Kingdom. God showed His goodness with the transformation of Saul of Tarsus, who became the Apostle Paul and how His goodness is available to all of us. F.F. Bruce nails it when he says, "With no conscious preparation, Paul found himself instantaneously compelled by what he saw and heard to acknowledge that Jesus of Nazareth, the crucified one, was alive after his passion, vindicated and exalted by God, and was now conscripting him into his service. There could be no resistance to this compulsion, no kicking out against this goad which was driving him in the opposite direction to that which he had hitherto been pursuing. He capitulated forthwith to the commands of this new master; a conscript he might be, but henceforth also a devoted and lifelong volunteer."[13] God's goodness can make us be a devoted lifetime volunteer in His goodness army. God can use any of us to share His goodness. Just like Paul, the Apostle, God can use us to change history. He used the twelve disciples, the Apostle Paul and many followers of Jesus. He wants to use you and I!

We already discussed in previous chapters that the presence of God reveals the glory of God and the glory of the Lord is actually the goodness of God. If we take a look at the Great Commission we are assured of the Lord's goodness following us because Jesus said that He will always be with us, even to the very end of the age. But the only condition given is that we must go and make disciples of all nations. Let us go, therefore, and release the goodness of God to every tongue, tribe and nation. We will witness the glory of God just as Moses did and experience how the goodness of God will follow us all the days of our lives, as with David. We, too, can join Paul in releasing God's goodness to the nations.

---

13 Bruce, F.F. *Paul Apostle of the Heart Set Free*. Grand Rapids: Wm. B. Eerdmans, 1977. pg 75.

REFLECT	We are to preach the good news (gospel) of Jesus. What incredible news He has for us! He loves us! He died for our sins! He came that we might have a relationship with Him, God the Father and God the Holy Spirit. That is good news!
EXPECT	God to bring people across your path that He wants to hear the good news, be healed, forgiven, loved and the like. He is a good God full of goodness. Who has God brought across your path to show His goodness to? As you have read this book, you have seen and received the goodness of God; now you can release the goodness of God.

Receiving God's Goodness Personally

The way to begin to receive the goodness of God is to receive the good news of the gospel of the Kingdom of God. Jesus Christ is the good news. He is King of the Kingdom. How do I receive Jesus Christ as my Lord and Savior you ask?

First, the Bible says that, "For all have sinned and fall short of the glory of God" (Romans 3:23). The first step to receive God's good news is to repent. In Mark 1:15 Jesus declared, "...The time is fulfilled, and the kingdom of God is at hand. Repent, and believe in the gospel." Repentance or repenting is a decision, a choice. So repenting is admitting to God that you have been living by your own plans and desires and now you are repenting (changing your mind) and are going to live God's way. You will turn from your sin and turn to God and submit to His plan for your life.

Secondly, after we repent we believe. What do we have to believe? Romans 10:8-10 states, "But what does it say? 'The word is near you, in your mouth and in your heart' (that is, the word of faith which we preach): that if you confess with your mouth the Lord Jesus and believe in your heart that God has raised Him from the dead, you will be saved. For with the heart one believes unto righteousness, and with the mouth confession is made unto salvation." If you believe Jesus Christ died for your sins and rose from the dead you can be saved! If you believe that in your heart you can become a Christian.

Thirdly, after you have repented and believed you can confess Jesus is your Lord. The word confess means "to say the same as." So you begin to confess what you believe the Bible says about what God says about you. If you confess with your mouth that Jesus is your Lord and believe God has raised Him from the dead...you will be saved!

Lastly, it is important to live what you believe. It is important to receive Christ into your life as your Lord and Savior. Then, it is important to be baptized in water. In Mark 16:15,16 says, "And He said to them, 'Go into all the world and preach the gospel to every creature. He who believes and is baptized will be saved; but he who does not believe will be condemned." It is important to find a Bible-believing church where you can become a member of a Christian family.

If you would like to receive Jesus Christ as your Lord and Savior, you can pray this prayer right now:

Dear God the Father,

I confess I am a sinner and need your forgiveness. I believe Jesus Christ, your Son died in my place on the cross and paid the penalty for my sin. And I believe Jesus rose from the dead. I repent and turn from sin and accept Jesus Christ as my personal Lord and Savior. I commit my life to you God and ask that the Holy Spirit would take control and help me live the Christian life. Than you for loving and accepting me as your child God. In Jesus Name, Amen.

If you have prayed this prayer from your heart and became God's child, please contact me at danhammerministries.org.

About the Author

Dr. Dan C. Hammer is a servant leader and a visionary with a passion to reach people with The Gospel of Jesus Christ. He loves to equip the saints to do the work of the ministry. Dan is the President of Seattle Bible College, Chancellor of Wagner Leadership Institute Seattle and a member of the United States Coalition of Apostolic Leaders. He has ministered in many nations.

He has a Bachelor of Theology from Seattle Bible College and a Masters and Doctorate from Bakke Graduate University.

Dan and his wife Terry planted Sonrise Christian Center in 1986 and are the senior pastors there in Everett, Washington. They have two grown married sons and a grown daughter. They have five grandchildren and live in Everett, Washington.

Made in the USA
Charleston, SC
29 October 2015